Praise for
Be Light

"Sammy Rodriquez is *light*. In this darkening hour in the world, God has raised up a godly man who is passionate spiritually, blessed intellectually, and gifted in leading masses of people. Through his book *Be Light,* he calls us to know what we believe, to stand for it courageously, and to change the world! Get this book. Share it with others. Let's change the world together."

—DR. RONNIE FLOYD, president, Southern Baptist Convention
and senior pastor, Cross Church

"I believe God's hand is on Sam Rodriguez as a prophet to our generation, and his message in *Be Light* comes at a time when the world we live in seems dark in so many ways. Delivered in thirty short, easy-to-read chapters, his insights, thoughts, and prophetic words will inspire you to be light."

—ROBERT MORRIS, founding senior pastor at Gateway Church
and best-selling author of *The Blessed Life, The God I Never Knew,*
and *Truly Free*

"As my friend Sammy Rodriguez passionately shares, our mandate as believers in Jesus Christ is to be light in this dark world—together becoming a shining 'city set on a hill that cannot be hidden.' His use of Scripture, scientific facts, and profound reflections will challenge you to pierce the darkness and radiate God's love and grace. Light exposes danger and reveals the best way. As we allow the light of Jesus to shine through us, we will bring glory to Him and hope to a world in great need."

—JAMES ROBISON, founder and president of LIFE Outreach
International and founder and publisher of *The Stream*

"What a book! Sam Rodriguez is definitely one of those few voices God raises for a generation. His clarity, insight, and passion leave no doubt he has heard from heaven. Even though we know darkness is increasing, the light of the church will arise far higher and brighter. This book will only cause the 'great light' to shine brighter and brighter to those sitting in darkness."

—PHIL PRINGLE, founder and president of C3 Church International and senior minister of C3 Church, Sydney, Australia

"Sammy Rodriguez is a dynamic leader. His influence impacts other leaders, both spiritually and politically. Yet his compassion touches the hurting, the marginalized, and the underrepresented. His message is compelling. He does not just articulate problems; he also gives solutions. His book, *Be Light,* is a must-read if you are tired of the darkness. Share it with your friends and help turn on the light."

—DR. ALTON GARRISON, assistant general superintendent, Assemblies of God USA

"Sam Rodriquez is a genius and a kind of prophet to our time. When he speaks, the world shakes and I listen. The truth is, you can't afford to not read this book."

—JOHNNIE MOORE, president, The KAIROS Company

BE LIGHT

Shining God's Beauty, Truth, and Hope into a Darkened World

SAMUEL RODRIGUEZ

Foreword by Roma Downey

WATERBROOK

Be Light

Trade Paperback ISBN 978-1-60142-818-9
Hardcover ISBN 978-1-60142-816-5
eBook ISBN 978-1-60142-817-2

Published in the United States by WaterBrook Multnomah, an imprint of the Crown Publishing Group, a division of Penguin Random House LLC, New York.

WATERBROOK® and its deer colophon are registered trademarks of Penguin Random House LLC.

The Library of Congress has cataloged the hardcover edition as follows:
Names: Rodriguez, Samuel, 1969- author.
Title: Be light : shining God's beauty, truth, and hope into a darkened world / Samuel Rodriguez.
Description: First Edition. | Colorado Springs, Colorado : WaterBrook Press, 2016. | Includes bibliographical references.
Identifiers: LCCN 2016002844 (print) | LCCN 2016005329 (ebook) | ISBN 9781601428165 (hardcover) | ISBN 9781601428172 (electronic)
Subjects: LCSH: Christian life.
Classification: LCC BV4501.3 .R644 2016 (print) | LCC BV4501.3 (ebook) | DDC 248.4—dc23
LC record available at http://lccn.loc.gov/2016002844

Printed in the United States of America
2017

10 9 8 7 6 5 4 3

SPECIAL SALES
Most WaterBrook books are available at special quantity discounts when purchased in bulk by corporations, organizations, and special-interest groups. Custom imprinting or excerpting can also be done to fit special needs. For information, please e-mail specialmarketscms@penguinrandomhouse.com or call 1-800-603-7051.

To my two gifts, Liam and Landon Samuel.
You changed my life and soon, in Christ,
you will change the world.

Contents

Foreword

Go ahead.

Strike a candle in a pitch black room.

The room can be the size of a baby's nursery or the size of a whole city block; it doesn't matter. In the blink of an eye, you'll be reminded of the power of a single, flickering flame.

No sea of darkness—no matter how intense—is any match for a tiny bit of light.

A midnight fire can be seen from outer space.

A single match can be seen for miles.

In fact, imagine that single match doubled and then doubled again. The light blazes even brighter with every added flame. Soon it's fifty people—then a hundred, all with their candles held high. Before you know it, the darkness is fully overcome by the light.

Jesus must have been thinking of this when He told His followers, "You are the light of the world. A city on a hill cannot be hidden" (Matthew 5:14).

Of a million possible analogies, He chose to call his followers "light." You might say He called them to be "light workers."

For my entire adult life, I've made being a "light worker" my personal and professional mission. I've always believed that *it's more powerful to light a candle than to curse the darkness.*

For my husband, Mark Burnett, and myself, we've realized our mission as "light workers" by producing content that families can watch together.

Content that lifts people up and inspires them to press on.

Content that reminds the world of stories that reveal the best in us.

Content that celebrates all that is good about our sometimes dark world.

We've also had the privilege of telling the story of Jesus—the ultimate "light worker"—on the History Channel through *The Bible,* on NBC through *A.D. The Bible Continues,* and on big screens around the world through *Son of God* and *Ben Hur.*

What a privilege it is to be a "light worker."

In the life and ministry of our dear friend, the Rev. Samuel Rodriguez, we have always found inspiration and a kindred spirit.

He's a "light worker" too (like few we've ever met).

He is a beautiful reminder to us all that when we share the message of Jesus, the candles of others are lit and more and more darkness is driven out of our world.

Our prayer is that this excellent book will inspire millions—including you—to *Be Light.*

> —Roma Downey, producer, celebrated actress, president
> and chief content officer at *LightWorkers Media*
> (a division of MGM Studios)

Be Light!

When light stands next to darkness, light always wins!

Let there be light!

It is not a coincidence that the first time the universe heard the uttered words of God, the message was not "let there be joy," "let there be peace," or even "let there be love." The voice of the Sovereign, the Divine, the Glorious said, "Let there be light."

God always begins by turning the lights on.

Life requires light.

Faith requires light.

We cannot deny we live in dark times. Some argue that we live in the blackest hour, darkened by sin, immorality, moral relativism, spiritual apathy, cultural decadence, infanticide, racism, pornography, poverty, false prophets, watered-down preaching, hypocrisy, unbridled consumerism, voyeurism, materialism, secular tyranny, religious extremism, terror, discord, division, strife, hatred, violence, jealousy, intolerance, and unbelief.

Did I miss anything?

Yet, while we cannot deny the canopy of disillusionment hovering upon our current day and age, there exists an undeniable physical and spiritual reality poised to serve as the impetus igniting hope, exposing love, and reintroducing grace. What might that be?

Simply stated, *when light stands next to darkness, light always wins!*
Jesus, while speaking to His followers, said,

A city on a hill cannot be hidden. Neither do people light a lamp and
put it under a bowl. Instead they put it on its stand, and it gives light to
everyone in the house. In the same way, let your light shine before men,
that they may see your good deeds and praise your Father in heaven.
(Matthew 5:14–16)

Joyce Smith did not just embrace this truth; she lived it out. On January 19,
2015, Joyce ran into a hospital room that was the quintessential corridor of darkness. The horrific reality was that her fourteen-year-old son, John, was dead.

A few hours prior, young John, accompanied by two other friends, had
played on top of Lake Sainte Louise in Missouri. Warm temperatures had
thawed the ice, providing a precarious circumstance that led to the three boys
falling into a frozen lake. While the other boys escaped the freezing water, John
did not emerge. His body was discovered fifteen minutes later—no pulse, life-
less . . . and darkness prevailed over the face of the deep.

Immediately, first responders rushed John to the nearest hospital, Saint
Joseph West, where the head emergency-room doctor, Kent Sutterer, stood waiting with his team. Approximately one dozen physicians, technicians, nurses,
and paramedics worked for another twenty minutes to no avail.

Later Dr. Sutterer wrote in a personal letter recording the event, "The boy
had remained pulse-less for forty minutes—plus transportation time—the better part of an hour." After attempts to raise the boy's temperature failed, Dr.
Sutterer determined the time had arrived to declare John Smith dead. He asked
to bring the boy's mother into the room.

And darkness prevailed over the face of the deep.

Joyce Smith rushed to her son's bedside. Seeing his gray and motionless
body, Joyce refused to embrace the darkened reality, to acknowledge that her
son was gone. At a recent Bible study class she had been instructed to believe in

a God who can do what He says He can do. Joyce had walked into an emergency room filled with darkness, but she exposed the light of faith, hope, and love. Without hesitation, Joyce opened her mouth, raised her voice, and said, "Lord, Holy Spirit, just give me back my son!"

In other words, "Let there be light!"

God's Spirit empowers us to go from existing in the natural to experiencing the supernatural.

Darkness was met with the brightness of faith, hope, and love. Instantly, a technician said, "We've got a pulse!" The atmosphere shifted; the room now filled with the light of joy and peace. Dr. Sutterer wrote, "That boy's heart was jump-started by the Holy Spirit listening to the request of a praying mother. . . . I know that God has given us a gift. . . . I was privileged to witness a miracle."[1]

Since then I've met John Smith and had the privilege of speaking to a healthy, healed, holy, happy young man. I asked him, "Do you realize that you died?"

"Yes sir," he responded.

"Why? Why did God give you back your life?" I asked.

"Because God has a great purpose for me," John answered.

What's John's purpose? Simply stated, I believe it's like your purpose and mine, to Be Light. We all go through trials, tribulations, and tests. The egregious and extreme canopy of darkness, which is death itself, may not be what we have individually confronted. Nevertheless, we have all, without exception, confronted darkness—be it spiritual, physical, in relation to our finances, in our families, or in our thoughts. To a great degree, we are all survivors of moments and seasons of darkness.

Yet here we still are. Why? For the same reason John Smith breathes today: God has a great purpose for you and me.

This book serves that very purpose: to expose the light that God has deposited, equipping us with the necessary spiritual and intellectual tools, not to fail or just survive, but to thrive. This book will engage, empower, and enrich you to Be Light, to shine, and to change your world. For we know for certain that "a city on a hill cannot be hidden. Neither do people light a lamp and put it under a bowl."

In other words, if you have the light, don't hide it. Let it shine!

Our challenge is to remove the bowl of apathy, complacency, acquiescence, and fear and once again lay claim to the lamp stand of righteousness so that we may shine before all people.

I am compelled to ask, what or who is trying to hide your light? In your life, what is the name of the proverbial bowl? For we cannot deny that there exists a spiritual battle to turn off your light.

Forget Harry Potter and Hogwarts! Based on what the Bible tells us, we know there are real spirits attempting to place a bowl on our light and fill us with darkness. The spirit of Pharaoh is alive, holding people captive in the Egypt of bondage and fear.

The spirit of Goliath still lives, mocking and intimidating the children of God.

The spirit of Jezebel still makes men and women hide in caves because of sexual perversion and manipulation.

The spirit of Absalom is dividing homes, churches, and relationships.

The spirit of Herod is killing the young through abortion, violence, infanticide, poverty, and sex trafficking—murdering dreams and vision.

Yet I have news for you. There is a Spirit more powerful than all these spirits combined! To Be Light requires acknowledgement that the most powerful Spirit alive today is not the spirit of Pharaoh, Goliath, Jezebel, Absalom, or Herod. The most powerful Spirit on our planet is the Holy Spirit of Almighty God, the Spirit of the Word that became flesh, the eternal Light that pushed back darkness with grace and love:

In the beginning was the Word, and the Word was with God, and the Word was God. He was with God in the beginning. Through him all things were made; without him nothing was made that has been made.

In him was life, and that life was the light of all mankind. The light shines in the darkness, and the darkness has not overcome it. (John 1:1–5, NIV 2011)

So to every narrative and spirit that exists for the purpose of obstructing our God-given purpose and hiding His grace-filled light in each and every one of us, I say the following:

- For every Pharaoh there must be a Moses.
- For every Goliath there must be a David.
- For every Nebuchadnezzar there must be a Daniel.
- For every Jezebel there must be an Elijah.
- For every Herod there must be a Jesus. And . . .
- For every devil that rises up against you, there is a mightier God who rises up for you!

It is time to remove the bowl.

It is time to throw off whatever life or hell has placed upon your light.

It is time to join me on a thirty-day journey of information and inspiration. This journey will not just inspire you, but it will also equip you to Be Light. For at the end of the day it takes

- conviction to repent,
- courage to speak truth,
- holiness to see God,
- faith to move mountains,
- love to change the world, and
- light to push back darkness.

For when light stands next to darkness, *light always wins*.

— • —

This book is centered on two powerful declarations: "Let there be light" and "You are the light of the world." The first pronouncement releases the power of light into the void. The second proclaims that we are creatures who are generative and reflective of an everlasting light.

We know that light fills our universe and that darkness always threatens. Yet we have a truth that has already been declared about us and that helps us solve the riddle of existence as it gives us definition and purpose: you are the light of the world. This sentence is a life metaphor that affirms a deep truth about every one of us: there is an inextinguishable light within each of us, a light that can penetrate and even eliminate the darkest places.

How do we embody light? If we are to Be Light, we must first understand its remarkable complexities. This book challenges you to take thirty days to begin living, even thriving, as you discover your destiny to Be Light. We are embarking on a journey together to understand the nature of light—a mysterious, powerful force—its laws, its attributes, and its power. Along the way you will undoubtedly be surprised by the parallels we can draw between the light around us and the light that is in us. We can be certain that in the discovery that comes with the study of this eternal substance, we will find something eternal and true within ourselves.

— • —

This is a book about the light of the world and how those who name the name of Jesus get to represent Him—even to be the light. And this is also a book about light, that constant in our lives that flows from the sun and other heavenly bodies but also comes from man-made sources we control by flipping switches. Light makes our lives so pleasant—where would we be without it? Light chases darkness away. It makes our sight possible. Without light we are lost in a cold world.

In examining the properties of light, I have found many intriguing insights that help me understand what it means, spiritually, to Be Light. Like all facets of creation, light reveals clues about God and His characteristics, so understanding more about light helps us know more about Him. In the next twenty-nine chapters, we will discover some of the remarkable laws that govern light, and we'll consider the striking parallels we can draw to our own lives as we attempt to be lights in this world. We will also consider darkness, which is light's enemy that threatens to extinguish our power to bring the hope and life inherent to light.

Together as we journey through this book, we will look at the intriguing qualities of light. And we will assemble these qualities meaningfully into a spiritual matrix that guides us to become light in our world.

Rise Up and Be Light!

No one lights a lamp and puts it in a place where it will be hidden, or under a bowl. Instead they put it on its stand, so that those who come in may see the light.
—Luke 11:33, NIV, 2011

Be Light and Walk like Enoch

Be Light and Believe like Abraham

Be Light and Dress like Joseph

Be Light and Stretch like Moses

Be Light and Shout like Joshua

Be Light and Dance like David

Be Light and Fight like Gideon

Be Light and Pray like Daniel

Be Light and Build like Nehemiah

And Be Light and Live like Jesus!

Knowing Light

What you know is more important than what you feel.

L ight.

It is our universe's most mysterious, essential force. We measure all matter by it, but it has no mass. Scientists don't know what to call the time that was "prelight" and simply say that before there was light there was "only the void." Experts say that once light is gone, all life disappears.

Light, unlike sound, needs no medium to travel through and actually travels fastest in a vacuum. It is the Usain Bolt of elements, speeding around the earth seven times in one second and containing a "cosmic speed limit" often expressed as $3\text{x}10^8$ m/s. It was through the study of light that we realized the universe is expanding, and as a result theories about the Big Bang materialized.

Even after thousands of years of study, experts still puzzle over light's most basic properties. Is it made up of particle-like photons or is it really a wave? The answer is yes—it is both. And even more baffling, when you test light for its particle properties, its wave dimensions disappear, and vice versa. Now that is mysterious. One way to consider light's duality is to imagine that when you peer through a telescope, wave after wave of light washes over it, but it is the individual photons that are absorbed by the neurons in your eyes.

Yet with all its dazzling qualities, its strictest definition is pretty boring: "Light is the visible part of the electromagnetic spectrum." *Yawn.* Then you realize that visible light is just a tiny part of a vast continuum, which ranges from radio waves that can be a mile long to gamma rays that are as small as an atom's nucleus, and you are even more amazed by this strange, luminous particle-wave.

Refraction, diffraction, interference, and dispersion are just some of the properties of this remarkable substance that we will consider as we try to understand the fullness of light and then transfer that complexity to our lives as "people of the light," those called to be the light of the world.

So here on day two of our journey, we will pause to understand some of the qualities and purposes of the light we are supposed to personify, knowing that in the chapters to come we will incrementally move forward to a new understanding of ourselves as the light of this world.

— • —

When we think of light, sunlight most often comes to mind, and no wonder. The sun holds over 99 percent of the solar system's mass, and to replicate its energy, you would have to explode 100 billion tons of dynamite every second! Sunlight has long been shown to have restorative power, with one study claiming that due to its "analgesic qualities," patients residing on the hospital's sunny side needed far less pain medication than others.[1] Sunlight produces vitamin D, and since the 1980s, bright light has been used as an effective therapy for depressive and circadian-rhythm disorders, such as seasonal affective disorder (SAD—an apt acronym). Light-therapy boxes are now covered by many insurance carriers, and Dragonskolan, an upper-secondary school in Umeå in Sweden's far north, uses high-intensity light to boost student performance during the deep midwinter gloom.[2]

Sun worship is as old as humankind, with followers referring to it as "the bestower of light and life to the totality of the cosmos; with his unblinking, all-seeing eye, he is the stern guarantor of justice, and the source of wisdom."[3]

First-century Roman philosopher Pliny the Elder echoed these sentiments when he wrote, "In the midst of these planetary gods moves the Sun, whose magnitude and power are the greatest. . . . He is glorious and preeminent, all-seeing and all-hearing."

Significantly, God spoke the words "Let there be light" before the sun was created, demonstrating that He, and not a created object, is the true Source of light and life. An affirmation of that truth is found in the depiction of heaven found in the book of Revelation. It says that heaven, the city of God, no longer needs the sun's or moon's illumination: "The city does not need the sun or the moon to shine on it, for the glory of God gives it light, and the Lamb is its lamp" (21:23).

Experts diligently investigate the first light of our universe, sometimes called primordial light, looking for "a baby picture of a very early universe." Light is generative like the sun, reflective like the moon, and sometimes both, like the earth (which produces the northern lights as a result of radiation from the sun). Or like you and me. If we already are—whether we feel like it or not—the light of the world, then we reflect God's light and transmit our own light as well.

The human body does, of course, reflect the sun's rays, and we also emit some infrared radiation, about nine megajoules, or the equivalent of two thousand calories a day (we are basically not hot enough to radiate visible light but are easily detected by night vision goggles and other instruments that detect infrared). Because we are receptacles and transmitters of light, then we must contain some of the same properties as light.

We will more fully discuss the reflective nature of light in a later chapter, but one fascinating aspect is called *albedo*, which is the reflective coefficient, or reflecting power of a surface. Albedos of typical materials in visible light range from up to 0.9 for fresh snow to about 0.04 for charcoal, one of the darkest substances.[4] All of us know that there are times in our lives when we are almost mirror-like in our reflection of God's light and love, and other instances—far too many for me—when we embody a lump of coal, absorbing every brilliant ray from God and giving out barely a flicker of illumination.

This book will give you practical, spiritual, emotional, and relational steps to help improve your "spiritual albedo," so that you can better reflect the light of life. The light of God is in the soul of every person. We do not want our light to be hidden under a bowl any longer, but we want it to be placed upon a stand for all to see.

— • —

Of course, visible light is only one aspect of the light of the world we are called to personify. Light is also "something that makes things visible or affords illumination." How often have we considered what we might illuminate? Are there people or issues that have been forgotten in the shadow of darkness that I need to bring to light?

God loves you too much to leave you in any state that is less than glorious.

Another of light's definitions is "to cause (the face, surroundings, etc.) to brighten, especially with joy, animation, or the like." Surely this definition of light relates directly to the call in our lives to Be Light. Just the thought of my grandbaby's smile causes my face to brighten, and I wonder how many times in a day we miss the opportunity to bring the joy of light to the life of another.

Light is also synonymous with learning. If we are to be true lights in this world, we want to think deeply, reason well, and know that while we are inherently limited in some ways as humans, we long to know ourselves, one another, and our God as fully as the light of knowledge will allow. We live to dispel ignorance and abhor superstition. We need the light of learning, the light of truth to suffuse our lives and radiate to others as well.

Indeed, the Bible says, "If we walk in the light, as he is in the light, we have fellowship one with another"[5] instead of living with the threat of violence between neighbors that befouls so many communities in our world today.

Light is a symbol of hope and protection. Lighthouses have long been beacons of warning to ships nearing land and dangerous shoals. A single light or candle in the window may be linked to an ancient symbol of welcome for a weary traveler looking for a place of refuge. Light can easily be taken for granted, but the fullness of the term reveals its complexity and value. From the visible light that illuminates our world to the light of knowledge, from the warming heat produced by light to the crime-reducing effect light can have, light is a unique, transforming force. What would we do without it? Better yet, what will we do with the light God has given us? How will we incarnate the power of light to touch darkness, overcome it, and shine brightly in the world?

The pages that follow will further reveal the remarkable laws and properties of light so that we might more fully understand the qualities of this substance we have been charged to become. As we develop a deeper understanding of the nature of light, we will become better at reflecting the Source and Maker of all light, the Light of life, the Lord Jesus Christ.

God fills every void. Wipes every tear. Breaks every chain. Washes every sin. Heals every heart. Delivers every captive. And all we have to do is call upon His name. He will respond . . . without exception!

===== Reflection =====

You Are in Christ . . .

"For in him we live and move and have our being." As
some of your own poets have said, "We are his offspring."
—Acts 17:28

Saved and not lost.

Delivered and not captive.

Healed and not sick.

Whole and not broken.

Free and not bound.

Filled and not empty.

Blessed and not cursed.

Accepted and not rejected.

Living and not dead!

So rise up and shine today!

Overcoming Darkness

When life throws you rocks, build an altar.

Darkness fills the universe, though we often think of light as far more common. In his dim work *Reaper Man,* author Terry Pratchett wrote, "Light thinks it travels faster than anything but it is wrong. No matter how fast light travels it finds the darkness has always got there first, and is waiting for it."[1]

We all know there are "dark forces" pulling families and communities apart in our country. We don't need to read Joseph Conrad's *Heart of Darkness* to know "the horror" that its protagonist discovers; spiritual and emotional darkness threatens our lives as surely as dark forces roam the heavenly realms. It is not the universe's darkness but the evil that seems to lurk in us all that looms to eclipse our light and prevent us from fulfilling our destiny as people of the light.

Studies clearly show that even literal darkness affects human beings, significantly increasing criminal behavior, which leads some to advocate for year-round daylight-saving time (DST). In one Stanford study, robbery rates decreased by 51 percent, reported murder by 48 percent, and rape by 56 percent during the hour of sunset prior to DST.[2] Police departments worldwide have taken notice, and many are using ambient light to help reduce crime.

To Be Light requires confronting and overcoming darkness in all its forms each day. This battle is rarely easy, but it can be won and is being won through God's faithful grace and power in our lives. Religion says, "Get rid of darkness

and light will shine." But the grace of Jesus says, "Let the light in and darkness
will flee."

The Bible clearly speaks of this battle between darkness and light. In one
of the most famous passages, we read,

> In the beginning was the Word, and the Word was with God, and the
> Word was God. . . . In him was life, and that life was the light of all
> mankind. The light shines in the darkness, and the darkness has not
> overcome it." (John 1:1, 4–5, NIV 2011)

That content-rich passage has a lot of truth to unpack, but for now let's
focus on the closing phrase, "The darkness has not overcome it." There is an
enduring promise and hope in that statement. Light has and will overcome
darkness. It is up to us to accept that promise and step out of the shadows into
the light. No matter our circumstances, no matter how bleak the future may
appear, we will stand in the knowledge that we *are* the light of the world, and
the light in us *will* overcome the darkness so that we can *shine* the light of truth
in our world.

Overcoming darkness sometimes involves willful accountability. For some,
this means having a sponsor whom we call when the darkness of alcoholism or
some other addiction tries to overpower us. For others, overcoming darkness
means walking away when we feel anger welling up inside us during a confron-
tation. Others must overcome the darkness of binge eating by regulating their
diet. Many of us are involved in dark relationships that effectively shut out the
light of our lives and negate our ability to shine the light of God. Darkness can
even be related to a work environment that forces us to deny our most deeply
held values, as the shadow of compromise infects our workplaces and our lives.

Some of us understand that darkness can originate in our family's history.
We may be looking back at generations who have engaged in dark behavior
that can predispose us to follow a tradition of wickedness. But we do not have
to succumb to the past. We have been promised light, and we are able to take

a stand, focus on our life goals, and forge a new tradition of light and life. The Word of God says, "Do not be anxious about anything, but in everything, by prayer and petition, with thanksgiving, present your requests to God" (Philippians 4:6). If we ask God to break the cycle of darkness in our family history, He is faithful to do it and will allow us to shine in a new way. We know we are fallen creatures who are drawn into darkness, which is all the more reason to resist, rebel against, and reject the sin that so easily besets us (see Hebrews 12:1). Sin eclipses the light of our lives.

Debt brings darkness to our finances.

Infidelity blots out true intimacy.

Depression shades our emotions.

Unforgiveness sullies our families.

We must choose light if we are to Be Light.

— • —

There are hundreds of stories that reveal the power of light to overcome darkness, and Sue Norton's tale of pain, forgiveness, and redemption is a classic example. In January of 1990, convicted criminal Robert Knighton broke out of a halfway house where he had been serving part of his sentence for a manslaughter conviction. A few days later he was on the run with two others, and—after already killing two—the dark trio pulled into the driveway of Richard and Virginia Denney's rented Oklahoma farmhouse. Richard Denney came out and asked the three if they needed help or directions, and they took him hostage, leading him at gunpoint inside the house. Knighton murdered the Denneys, stole their old truck, and took a paltry $61 in cash.

After all the killers were caught, Knighton was convicted and awaiting execution on death row in Oklahoma. What darkness must have filled his heart and cell as his days receded into a blackened past and his bleak future loomed like an evil, ever-present specter of death.

Then light came into Knighton's life in the form of Sue Norton, Richard

Denney's adopted daughter. Sue initially felt anger and hatred for the man who had taken her father's life, but she vowed to overcome that darkness and shine the light of forgiveness to a man who many said deserved none. Knighton was shocked that a family member began to write to him and then visit, telling him that she forgave him and hoped he would begin thinking and living differently.

Sue continued to embody the light of hope to Knighton for over ten years, and she actually asked the Oklahoma Pardon and Parole Board to have mercy upon her father's killer. The parole board rejected the plea for clemency, and Sue and others were there weeks later when Knighton was executed by lethal injection.

At the time Sue told reporters, "This is the first time in his life that he feels like he's doing something right. It took him this long to realize he spent over fifty of his years living totally against God." Perhaps Sue Norton's light penetrated a life of darkness. In his last words, Knighton said, "I'm sorry for all I've done." Then, speaking to his only friend in the world, he said to Sue, "I'll see you again someday. God bless you."

He took his last breaths minutes later but did not die in utter darkness. His tortured life was illumined by the light of a friendship unlike any he had ever known, a friendship kindled in the light of God.[3]

Sue Norton could easily have allowed the darkness of her father's brutal murder to fill her thoughts and life. Many in a circumstance like this have "died a second death" due to the loss of a loved one. Sadly, that is the power of darkness. It can hold us in a grip that seems inextricable but really is not. We have been given an inextinguishable light that cannot be overcome by any evil thing. It can illuminate any dark place and fill any heart with the hope and life that comes with His eternal light of forgiveness and grace.

— • —

Here on the third day of our thirty-day voyage toward the light, we must take an inventory of our lives and remove the darkness so that our light may shine.

We need to look deeply into our souls and ask God to find the darkness in us and confront it so that we can reflect His hope in the most bleak places and situations.

Where is there bitterness in relationships? Today we, as people of the light, will pick up the phone or visit a family member or former friend and have a conversation we may have been dreading, but one that can eliminate the darkness that has held us captive. Today we will remove an ongoing temptation from our daily lives. We will stop justifying actions that we know to be wrong. We will cut our ties with people and things that impede our light from shining.

"God is light; in him there is no darkness at all" (1 John 1:5). If there is no darkness in Him, then we need to draw close to Him to fully shine. Just as we would argue that our wills are most free as we move closer to God, so we would say that we better reflect the light of God as we draw near to Him.

We can take a step and do just that today. His light will burn away any darkness and cause a new, enduring light in us to shine out to others.

The Lamp of God Has Yet to Go Out

Samuel was sleeping in the Tabernacle near the Ark of
God.—1 Samuel 3:3, NLT

It's dark.

Darkness seems to be taking over.

Darkness seems to be growing.

We see darkness everywhere—the darkness of sin, relativism,
perversion, idolatry, bitterness, hatred, and apathy.

Yet here's the word: "The lamp of God has yet to go out!"

The light is still shining.

Christ is still on the throne.

His Word refuses to come back void.

His Spirit is still moving.

His name still makes demons tremble and sicknesses shrivel up,
and provokes the devil to flee.

The lamp has yet to go out!

So to the spirit of Babylon—idol worship and paganism.

To the spirit of Sodom and Gomorrah—sexual perversion and
immorality.

To the spirit of Capernaum—unbelief.

To the spirit of hatred, poverty, bitterness, strife, discord, relativism, and apathy, we pronounce the following:

The lamp of God has yet to go out!

Let us make a bold declaration: Darkness will not overcome light.
Darkness cannot penetrate light.

Light will always overtake darkness.

In Jesus's name.

We Emit What We Absorb

You are what you tolerate.

In a Berlin cemetery, just a few feet from the stones of the Brothers Grimm, is a marker for Gustav Kirchhoff, the nineteenth-century German physicist who would spend much of his life studying electricity, radiation, and light. While Grimms' fairy tales are renowned for their dark themes, Kirchhoff would reveal some fascinating properties of light. In particular, his "radiative transfer law" stands as a staple in physics classrooms across the world.

Greatly simplified, this law states that "the ability of an object to absorb radiation is also related to its ability to emit radiation." Further simplified, we could say absorption equals emission. Said another way, we emit what we absorb, minus what we retain.

As the light of the world, we are commanded to let our light shine, so understanding this principle and monitoring our light absorption, retention, and emission is critical to how well we are aligning our lives to this truth.

You will recall that we've already discussed a phenomenon called albedo, which is the reflecting power of a surface. As people of the light, we must work daily to improve our ability to reflect the light, love, and life that come from God. Yet we must first focus on what we absorb and how we retain that, and then we will emit a light that brings life and blessing to the world.

The key in reflecting the light of God is eliminating the focus on ourselves. When John the Baptist spoke of the Lord and announced, "He must increase, but I must decrease,"[1] he spoke a truth that applies to all of us who are determined to Be Light.

One of the first words we learn as infants is "mine," and we spend our lives battling our tendency to conform in a "me first" society. It is no wonder that God's first commandment given to Moses was, "You must not have any other god but me" (Exodus 20:3, NLT). It is also no wonder that King Herod killed every young male child in Bethlehem when he heard that another king had been born. Only one can sit on any throne, and only one can sit on the throne of our lives. And it cannot be you or me if we are to be the light of the world. We are our first "god" and must shift our focus so that we reflect the only true God and diminish the focus on ourselves.

Yet as the light of the world, we are more than just mirrors. We must reflect the light of God, but we also must absorb the light of His presence and teaching so that we can emit a light that is truly ours and not just a surface reflection of faith. Too often people learn the language of faith, even the traditions, but they are not fully absorbing and synthesizing the power of the light.

What we must activate is a spiritual version of photosynthesis, which is a complex natural process that involves more than a plant simply reflecting the light of the sun. Plants must absorb sunlight and synthesize it before they give off oxygen, which is a nutrient for other life forms.

In a comparable way, we followers of Christ must learn to absorb all the light that God has for us so that we can reflect some, retain some, and emit some.

— • —

Just as some of us reflect too much light without absorbing the correct amount, others can absorb too much and not reflect or emit enough. Science even has a term for an object that fails to reflect; it is called a "perfect blackbody." A perfect blackbody is one that absorbs all incoming light and does not reflect any at all.

The Bible says that to whom much has been given, much is required (see

Luke 12:48), and we have been given so much light. The light we receive from God is eternal, transforming, and powerful. We cannot simply absorb the love and light of God then fail to reflect and emit that light to the world around us.

Many spend time studying the Word of God, attending church services, perhaps meeting with small groups to discuss God's truth or listening to experts describe the many aspects of our faith. Yet we are born to be "rivers of life" and conduits of light and life.

We are born to absorb and then reflect God's light.

God knew you before you knew Him. He loved you before you loved Him. He chose you before you chose Him. He took the first steps.

Your move.

— • —

How does darkness prevent us from reflecting and emitting God's light?

There are several ways, but many of us are simply living in the shade, as though the light of the Son of God is not falling on us. It could be said of us that we are victims of a "spiritual eclipse."

We all are familiar with the phrase *solar eclipse,* where the moon fully or partially blocks or "occults" (an interesting word that science uses!) the sun's light. But the word *eclipse* also means to obscure anything, and the dark forces of this world can eclipse the light of God from our lives.

We all know that sin is the dark body that moves across the sky of our lives. It often grows imperceptibly, and then we find ourselves in the shadows of death, far from God. The Bible says that light has come into the world, but we loved darkness more than light. (See John 3:19.) All of us have some measure of the Light (God) that shines in the darkness within us to expose the evil in our hearts and turn us to the light. But we can love our dark ways, and we often ignore the gentle pleadings of the Lord and remain in darkness.

Another danger lurks in that if we begin to absorb darkness instead of light, that darkness will swallow up our light. Just as surely as we will reflect and emit the light of God when we are near Him, we will lose our ability to reflect light when we drift from Him and surround ourselves with darkness.

Darkness produces darkness. A black hole in space has such a strong gravitational pull that no light—not even a particle of electromagnetic radiation—can escape from it. Black holes are said to be so powerful that they deform the space-time continuum, and darkness will similarly deform our lives if we refuse to let light in.

Because our surroundings are so critical to our ability to Be Light, we must be intentional in choosing people of the light as friends. If it is true that "bad company corrupts good character" (1 Corinthians 15:33), then dark influences corrupt our light. If the Total Power Law states that when radiative power is falling on an object, some will be radiated, some absorbed, and some transmitted, then we can say that the opposite is true. When darkness is falling on us, we must decide to not absorb it but instead replace it with God's restorative light.

— • —

As we approach each day from now on, we will focus on doing all we can to absorb the blessing and goodness that comes from the Light of life and then emit that Light of grace to all around us.

Flashlight or Lamp?

> I have made you a light for the Gentiles, that you may bring
> salvation to the ends of the earth.—Acts 13:47

Jesus tells us that we are the light of the world, that a lamp must be placed on a stand to shine the light for all to see. But there is a problem. Many believers act more like a flashlight than a lamp. The difference is simple.

Flashlights shine for a moment, run on batteries, and are activated or turned off by a touch.

But the lamp produces constant light because it is plugged in, connected to the source.

Be a lamp! Stay connected to Christ, to His Spirit. As long as the Source produces power, as long as Christ is on the throne, your light will shine.

Increasing Our Internal Temperature

He who wrote the law with one finger
gives us grace with both hands.

We now turn from an emphasis on external radiation to an inward focus to learn how we might burn hotter and shine brighter as people of the light.

While German physicist Gustav Kirchhoff's focus was on how external radiation influenced objects, his countryman Max Planck was fascinated by objects that glowed red with heat. Internal radiation became his obsession.

In 1894, Planck was commissioned by electric companies to create light bulbs with maximum light output using minimal energy. Planck knew that the temperature of the body was a key part of his research. Planck would go on to win the Nobel Prize and make discoveries that led to the field now known as quantum physics. His theories also give us some remarkable principles about light that we can apply to our ongoing personal development as the light of this world.

One of the most fascinating elements of Planck's work relates to thermal radiation. Planck wrote that any matter with a temperature greater than absolute zero (that's −459 °F) emits thermal radiation. As temperatures rise, atoms collide and their kinetic energy begins to change. Light, of course, is the thermal energy we can see with the naked eye. If the object gets hot enough, we can see its light, but most objects' internal heat is so low that we need special instruments, like an infrared camera, to detect it.

The laptop I am working from emits several kinds of radiation. There is the visible light coming from the screen. In addition, there is the internal radiation that is infrared and makes the laptop warm to the touch. There is also electromagnetic radiation, radio waves that connect me to the wireless network and those that link me to the wireless mouse. There is even some nuclear radiation leaking out of the computer through the natural decay of atomic isotopes in the materials used to make the machine.

When we read of these principles, we think about how they might apply to our own lives. Perhaps our first (cynical) response is that we are sure we have met people who have reached an internal temperature of absolute zero and have achieved what scientists call the "ground state" or "the lowest point of internal energy." Let's face it, we all have had those moments when we are certain we have become so apathetic that not a single atom of our being collides with another, and if we radiate anything it is an isotope of hopelessness. It is no wonder that the ground state is also called the "vacuum state." Once we become cold, instead of radiating any light to others, we transform into human vacuums, ingesting everything around us instead of radiating the light of life. Even two superheated objects, when placed in a complete vacuum, radiate no heat, as there is no way for the heat to be transferred.

Science tells us that "the amount of thermal radiation emitted by an object depends on its internal temperature, area, and characteristics."[1] In being light, what can we do to increase our "surface temperature"? And what about our "area and characteristics"? We know that warmer objects emit more thermal radiation than cooler ones, so how do we increase our internal temperature so much that we glow with a light that shines through any darkness?

Nothing is more certain to increase our internal light and temperature than setting time aside each day to focus on God. It is no wonder that nuclear colliders use completely impermeable materials to shut out all objects to ensure that fusion will occur internally and produce power. We must have a time each day when we shut out the distractions of life that impede the creation of a spiritual fusion of our souls with God that will produce a similar power in us. If fusion is in fact "the act or process of fusing or melting together," then our time alone with God each day will generate more light and heat than any other single thing.

Just as daily physical exercise produces a healthy body, daily spiritual exercises produce an internal "heat" that is caused by the light of truth that comes only from God.

Many of us would never neglect our workout routines. They make us more physically fit and produce all kinds of healthy serotonin and dopamine for our brains, improving our mental states as well. Yet it is easy to put off our daily spiritual calisthenics and allow our internal temperature and light to dissipate. We need time with the One who is the Light of life so that His light will fuse with our own each day.

One of my favorite lines from the beautiful Christmas carol *Silent Night* is, "All is calm, all is bright." There is a calming brightness that comes when we dedicate a time of meditation and devotion to God each day. So it was that Moses's face shone after he was in God's presence.

We are told in Scripture to "put on all of God's armor so that [we] will be able to stand firm against all strategies of the devil. For we are not fighting against flesh-and-blood enemies, but against evil rulers and authorities of the unseen world, against mighty powers in this dark world" (Ephesians 6:11–12, NLT).

This armor must be put on each day, an intentional act to protect against darkness and insulate our internal heat from the cooling effects of evil. If we have true union with God, change must come. An authentic connection with God can't fail to make us more loving toward others. If He makes His face to shine upon us, we will never be the same.

— • —

Benedict of Nursia, who is sometimes called the father of Western monasticism, expressed a deep truth about daily meditation. He understood that it has the power to put all things in their proper perspective and order. He wrote, "The light of holy contemplation enlarges and expands the mind in God until it stands above the world. In fact, the soul that sees Him rises even above itself, and as it is drawn upward in His light all its inner powers unfold. Then, when it looks down from above, it sees how small everything is that was beyond its grasp before."[2]

Our time with God lifts us from the drudgery of our daily lives into the light of His presence, which illuminates the dark places in our lives as it brightens those places He already inhabits. The God who created the sun, which has an internal temperature that casts heat to our planet some 93 million miles away, can create in us an inner core of light that can touch lives wherever we go.

In addition to daily spiritual activities, we need to eliminate those things from our lives that inevitably bring down our internal temperature and ability to radiate light. Most of us know that tobacco use, poor diet, and lack of exercise are the top three issues that compromise physical health, but things get muddier when we speak of spiritual health. Yet just as surely as smoking leads to emphysema and cancer, a life without prayer leads to spiritual apathy, and a bad temper leads to conflict.

One of the things we need to learn in order to keep our internal temperature hot is to develop a positive personal narrative that replaces the deficit narrative that hampers so many of us. Too often we let circumstances or others limit what we believe we can do.

With the light of God, all things are possible. *All things.* "I can do all things through God who strengthens me" is a simple prayer that can be recited at any time and is sure to raise your internal temperature immediately.

Seek to eliminate those negative words you speak about yourself. Do not allow the words of others—no matter how long and how often they have been spoken about you—hamper what you know to be true: *you are God's child, a child of the light, and you must let your light shine in this world.*

Eliminate destructive relationships. Stop the habits that you know prevent you from your destiny. Consider a month away from the television or computer. Perhaps you too often take the easy way or tell less than the whole truth. All of these things reduce our "constant internal temperature" and our ability to bless others with our light.

Author Gary Hansen understands how life can get in the way of our daily devotion to God: "Sheer busyness can keep us from regular prayer, as demands sweep us along like a river. Some say we become 'human doings' instead of 'human beings.' Life feels at least slightly out of control, and we lose track of why we are doing what we are doing."[3]

Spending time with the Lord is an intentional act that keeps us from the river's sweeping power. It gets us out on the bank, where we can watch the river flow and decide if we want to take a new direction or perhaps seek out an entirely new river.

Chris Sutton was only seventeen when he was diagnosed with terminal, inoperable cancer and was not expected to live long. A family friend remembers visiting Chris during the last weeks of his life: "I entered the house and found Chris lying on a hospital bed in the family room with his mother by his side. He looked up as I came in and gave me an awesome smile. Then suddenly, as if reading my mind, he looked right at me and said, 'Don't worry about me. I'm going home to Jesus and I am not afraid.' His calmness and sense of joy took me by surprise. . . . Amazingly, Chris still seemed to radiate hope and light despite the fact that the cancer was destroying his body."

The same friend later added that Chris "continued to encourage the young people of the church to trust in Jesus and many came to believe because of him. . . . His Bible was engraved with the words, *'No fears, no regrets'* and that was how he lived."[4]

Chris Sutton displayed a maturity beyond his years. Consider the words used to describe him: *calm, hope, light.* Surely these are the words that we hope others will use to describe us one day. When we read the description of his "awesome smile," we think of those we have met who seem to radiate the love of God through their smiling eyes and faces.

Many of us have had the privilege of knowing people like Chris. Some would say they were "angels" and "too good for this world." In any case, they are people whose simple smiles transform as they reflect the light of God. Chris Sutton did not waste his time with empty things. He focused on loving others and surely had a greater impact than many who live well into their eighth decade.

— • —

Max Planck was ultimately successful in identifying the optimal temperature for a light bulb to reach maximum efficiency: 3,200 Kelvin. It is the most common temperature still used in today's light bulbs.

What is our "maximal efficient temperature"? While we are not likely to arrive at an exact constant that applies to each person, we can strive to increase our internal heat, eliminate cooling distractions, and fully glow with the light of God.

Stop Surviving, Start Thriving!

Jesus said, "The thief's purpose is to steal and kill and destroy. My purpose is to give them a rich and satisfying life."—John 10:10, NLT

There's a difference . . .

Between the desert and the promised land.

Between life and a blessed life.

Between "I'm okay" and "I am more than a conqueror."

Between enough and more than enough.

Between full and overflowing.

Between making it and overcoming.

Between existing and shining.

Between rhetoric and action.

Between speaking faith and bearing fruit.

Between having a dream and living out a vision.

Paul said, "In all these things we are more than conquerors through him who loved us" (Romans 8:37). And, "Now all glory to God, who is able, through his mighty power at work within us, to accomplish infinitely more than we might ask or think" (Ephesians 3:20, NLT).

Jesus was not born to a virgin, baptized in the Jordan, crucified on the cross, raised from the tomb, and ascended to heaven so that you and I would just *survive*.

Absolutely not.

Jesus Christ, the son of Mary, the carpenter's son, came down not so you and I would just make it, not so you and I would just get by. He came down so you and I would have life in abundance.

God wants you to live, not just exist. He wants you to thrive, not just survive. He wants you to be a blessing and not just ask for blessings.

Heaven touched earth so we would go from failure to survival to thriving.

You have survived.

Now it's time to thrive!

The Law of Reflection

God does not look for those who
have it all. He looks for those who
are willing to surrender it all.

In the time of Christ, mathematician Heron of Alexandria used a geometrical method to show that the path taken by a ray of light reflected from a plane (flat) mirror is shorter than any other reflected path between the source and point of observation.

Say what?

Heron's ancient observation led to a property of light called the law of reflection. In simpler terms the law says that the direction of incoming light (called the incident ray) and the direction of outgoing light reflected (the reflected ray) make the same angle.

Heron's ancient observation and subsequent law of reflection provide us with unique insights we can apply as people called to Be Light.

One of the remarkable features of this law is its unrelenting consistency. Change the angle of the incoming light, and the reflected ray becomes its twin. Predictability and consistency might be boring to some, but as children of the light, we should strive to develop the qualities that transform us into consistent, trusted people.

We generally take the reliability of light for granted. A flip of a switch, and we know what follows—instant illumination. How can we become more constant? What do we need to change today to become a more perfect mirror to reflect the light of God? What are the "incident rays" now falling into our lives, and how will we reflect them?

— • —

Reflected light has always been a source of great wonder. We can only imagine the first time a man or woman peered into the water and saw his or her astonished face staring back. In Greek mythology, Narcissus liked what he saw so much that he was condemned to view his handsome image forever.

Some say we have been obsessed with our images ever since. A recent survey found that the average woman in America spends fifty-five minutes every day in front of a mirror.[1] (I am really hopeful that the researchers' methods were flawed!) Mirrors have always been associated with the soul, presumably because of the idea that when we see our reflection, we are looking at a "second self" of sorts. Superstition says that a shattered mirror brings with it the pall of seven luckless years. The evil queen looks into her mirror daily, and it speaks words that reflect her egotistical, invidious soul. In some cultures mirrors are covered when someone dies because according to some superstitions, a mirror can trap the soul of a dead person. Another fable says that vampires and witches will never see themselves in mirrors because they have no souls.

A mirror is "an object that reflects light in such a way that . . . the reflected light preserves many or most of the detailed physical characteristics of the original light. This is different from other light-reflecting objects that do not preserve much of the original wave signal other than color and diffuse reflected light."[2] For people called to Be Light, we hope to mirror the Light of the world, the eternal God whose perpetual light brings hope to all. The better we can preserve "the detailed. . .characteristics of the original light," the more the true Light that can never be extinguished will shine. So we must strive to be pure mirrors free from flaws and defects.

As the law of reflection makes clear, as the "incident ray" of God's light falls upon us, we—as mirrors—will produce a "reflection ray" that projects God's image to the world. By doing so we help others and ourselves to better know our true identity. Mirrors can only reveal so much, but we as "living mirrors" are able to allow God's light to reveal deep truths to our own hearts and those of others.

The image that comes to mind is a "house of mirrors" that I remember from carnivals and big-tent circuses from my youth. As I walked through this attraction, I viewed many mirrors, each reflecting a different crazy image. Sometimes my head would be huge, bending and twisting, with saucer-sized eyes and a smile that was an immense Cheshire Cat grin. In the next mirror I was impossibly thin and tall. Then I was squat and round.

While the house of mirrors was silly entertainment, I can see now that it parallels the fact that nearly all of us have lingering distorted images of ourselves. Nearly everyone I get to know sees himself or herself far differently than others do. So many women are plagued by image inadequacy. They feel they are ugly or fat or old or blemished by the inability to meet some social expectation. Men often have similar feelings. But beyond these physical references, most have a deeper problem with self-image, as they have allowed life circumstances and others to convince them that they just don't measure up.

There also is an emotional and psychological house of mirrors that can reflect a distorted image of our true self. Some see themselves as complete failures, but most feel guilty about the past. Others are stuck in emotional, intellectual, or spiritual neutral, unfulfilled and just drifting along. Perhaps they have been abused in some way and the scars are so deep that their self-image is flawed. Hurtful words spoken by someone we respect can surely deform our self-esteem and lead us to develop misguided images of ourselves.

Physical and emotional suffering often produce distorted views of self, and we need to look afresh into the mirror of God's true light to see who we truly are. I am not advocating some facile self-help approach that promises to wish away the past or deep feelings of hurt simply by declaring that they do not exist.

Instead I am saying that no life is beyond hope because no life is beyond the reach of a loving, forgiving, redeeming God. Just as light reveals the true form of those things around us, God's pure, true light alone uncovers the fullness of who we are. And God never wavers about our worth. He loves us and knows us with all our physical, mental, spiritual, and emotional baggage, and He says there is no lack, no gap, no insufficiency that He cannot rectify. In truth, all has been forgiven; all is redeemed.

If we do not see it, then our mirror is distorted, and we need a better one. This book is just an imperfect tool in His perfect hands, but He can use it to hold up a mirror to the reality that comes only from Him—all else is a distortion.

For this reason, we must strive to be more like God so that we can be used as His perfectly functioning mirror of truth to others. We must be those who seek out the broken ones, the forgotten and hurting ones, the physically and spiritually impoverished ones, the ones imprisoned by lies of imperfect mirrors; and we must hold up the eternal image of God, whose light shines through us to bring healing and restoration. We are the light of the world, so our words of gentle affirmation must replace the words of hatred and pain that have marred many lives. Our actions will help others see that they can walk in the light of newness and leave the darkness of a fractured self-image behind.

Noah saw a rainbow. Moses saw a burning bush. Jacob saw a ladder. Ezekiel saw a wheel. Peter saw a sheet descend. When you walk with God, you will see what you have never seen before.

As a father I often consider the awesome privilege and responsibility of reflecting God to my children. I know I am supposed to reflect God to them by being

- loving, gracious, and kind;
- a provider and protector;
- humble, gentle, and wise;
- righteous, just, and blameless.

And the list goes on. Now that is pressure!

I know I will be imperfect in reflecting these and many other facets of our infinite God, but what a privilege to have the ability to engender in them those bright qualities of a loving God.

As people called to Be Light, we have that same responsibility and privilege to reflect God to our spouse, coworkers, and all others.

— • —

One of the elements of the law of reflection is that between every incoming and outgoing ray of light, there is the "normal line," the perpendicular line from which we measure the angles of the two rays of light. I would suggest that when it comes to reflecting the light of God, it is easy to be seduced by the normal line, which always tries to pull us from a sharp, unique angle to that dull, average place others call normal.

Normal is overrated! It's a social creation often used as a yardstick to measure others and even control them. Normal people rarely shape history.

It was not "normal" for a leader to call for revolutionary change, yet demand that nonviolence be the vehicle to bring that change. It was not "normal" for a preacher to focus on God's love and forgiveness so relentlessly that thousands packed stadiums to hear his words of hope. Both Martin Luther King Jr. and Billy Graham were not "normal" men; they refused to rely on others' views of normal behavior and instead reflected a light that cut through the darkness of prejudice and separation from God and brought new promise.

The pursuit of normal is like chasing the wind. The moment you are sure you have settled into the fleeting comfort that comes with normalcy, a "thought leader" will reveal a "new normal" to which you will be asked to conform. Normal people don't challenge the status quo. Normal people are conventional. They go with the flow and rarely make waves.

But there is nothing normal about light. It defies definition and refuses to be confined. People of the light must resist the "normal line" that divides incoming and outgoing light and aspire to the extraordinary, the transformational.

— • —

Understanding the law of reflection will help us incorporate additional aspects of Being Light into our everyday routines. We will think more fully about how well we are functioning as mirrors of God's light and truth and will work to eliminate anything from our lives that would make His light less brilliant as it reflects off of us. We will reinforce the truth about who we are at the core and not allow a psychological or physical house of mirrors to destroy our personhood. And we will also resist that "normal line" that tends to define us by society's standards rather than God's high calling.

Reflection

Who Are We?

> You are the light of the world. A city on a hill cannot be
> hidden.—Matthew 5:14

The question must be asked: Who are we? Are we, as the church, just another institution in society? Are we another religious faith narrative competing in the marketplace of ideas? Are we feel-good machinery for the spiritually impaired? Are we an antiquated conduit for a set of irrelevant values no longer applicable in the world of Facebook, iPads, Twitter, Instagram, and YouTube?

How this generation responds will determine whether in this generation light will overcome darkness.

Who are we? We must respond with clarity, conviction, and courage to the following:

We are the light of the world (Matthew 5:14).

We are a city on a hill (Matthew 5:14).

We are people of the Word (1 Kings 8:56).

We are salt and light (Matthew 5:13–16).

We are prophetic and not pathetic.

We are disciples, witnesses, and Christ followers (Matthew 28:16–20).

We are apostles, prophets, evangelists, pastors, and teachers (Ephesians 4:11).

We are children of the Cross (Romans 8:17), fruit of the empty tomb (John 12:24), and a product of the upper room (Acts 2).

We are the redeemed of the Lord (Psalm 107:2).

We are the sheep of His pasture (Psalm 100:3).

We are forgiven, free, and favored.

We are called and chosen (1 Peter 2:9).

We are warriors and worshipers (Psalm 144:1).

We are world changers and history makers (Mark 16:15).

We are the church of Jesus Christ, and the gates of hell shall not prevail against us (Matthew 16:18).

Refraction: Bending Light and Bending Lives

The size of your praise is proportional
to the hell God freed you from.

I n 1665, a young scientist studying at Cambridge University was very interested in learning all about light and colors. One bright sunny day, he darkened his dorm room and made a tiny hole in his window shutter, allowing a
single beam of sunlight to pierce into the room. He then took a glass prism and
placed it in the sunbeam. The result was a spectacular multicolored band of
light just like a rainbow.

The young man was named Isaac Newton, and he had just demonstrated
a new property of light related to what we know as refraction. Refraction is the
bending of light (it also happens with sound, water, and other waves) as it
passes from one transparent substance into another.

As we close out week one of our Be Light experiment, we will see how light
responds when it confronts certain obstacles. Its behavior is unexpected but
holds within it some strategies that we can employ as we work to become the
light of the world. Just as light bends and separates when it strikes water and
glass, we can learn to do the same when we meet an obstacle, and in the process
see the fullness of God's glory refracted through us—living prisms waiting to
receive the light from above.

Prisms work on the principle of refraction, which is Latin for "to turn aside
or bend." As light enters a transparent medium of greater density than air, the

laws of physics dictate that the beam undergoes a slight bending. Because we want God's light to "travel through us," we need to be "transparent mediums" that allow the light to pass through us. If not, the light will be diffused and will not be visible to others. Author Vera Nazarian reminds us that "in the kingdom of glass everything is transparent, and there is no place to hide a dark heart."[1]

Transparency is a quality that many of us aspire to but find difficult to achieve. Webster defines *transparent* as "having the property of transmitting rays of light through its substance so that bodies situated beyond or behind can be distinctly seen." Those words seem to be written directly to us as people called to Be Light. Science tells us: "Objects that transmit light are either translucent (scattering the transmitted light) or transparent (not scattering the transmitted light)."[2] We must be transparent to fully transmit God's light and so better reveal that which is around us.

Yet transparency is demanding. We are reluctant to reveal our deepest selves because we are sure others will find us wanting. It is far easier to cloak our weaknesses than expose ourselves to the world, but the courageous ones, the ones who know they have nothing more to lose, those who have matured beyond where judgments can reach, are the people who can be transparent and transmit light more fully. Transparency is a quality that needs practice and nurturing to become part of who we are. If we allow ourselves to be fully known, we will find a new freedom with God and others.

Yet even with transparent mediums there is a "bending" that occurs when God's light passes through us. Science says one reason light bends in a prism is because there are impurities in even the finest glass. We all have our own impurities that cause the light of God to slow down and bend when it reaches us. This bending by refraction makes it possible for there to be lenses, magnifying glasses, prisms, and rainbows. Even our eyes depend upon this bending of light. Without refraction, we wouldn't be able to focus light onto our retinas.

For us, this bending is part of the process of God working in us to bring us to a place where we can be used more effectively. Our knees bend as we kneel in worship to God. We bend our heads forward in prayer. Sometimes our very lives are bent by the weight of sorrow we endure. But God is there, and His burden is easy. He gives rest to the heavy laden who are bent low by suffering and hardship.

One of the most remarkable aspects of the prism is that when light passes through, the prism reveals the full color spectrum. This phenomenon is surely supposed to be replicated in people like us who are called to be the light of the world. So often it seems that others perceive people of faith as uniform, mono-chromatic, or one dimensional. Certainly the God we serve is kaleidoscopic in His variation and bounty. It is a high calling indeed to be an instrument through which God reveals the various "wavelengths" that represent Him, from the deep indigo of violet to the burnished crimsons of red and all in be-tween. The light of God may appear to be a single beam of white light, but when it passes through the prisms of His people, its full complexity and beauty are revealed.

In its simplest form, a prism is an obstacle to light and slows the light rays down as it changes their course. As the light of God is transmitted through us, it will confront obstacles, and we will as well. But to us these impediments are not deterrents but provide the means by which we refract light and expose the fullness of God's color spectrum in and through us. In other words, obstacles do not deter us but provide an opportunity for the fullness of God to be revealed.

Joni Eareckson Tada is a perfect example of a woman who is able to use an obstacle as a mechanism to reveal God's wondrous nature. Years ago as a teen-ager, Joni broke her neck diving into shallow water, and, as she describes it, "permanent and total paralysis smashed me up against . . . God." Joni's aston-ishing attitude of joy and hope have been an inspiration for many. She has been "bent" by life's circumstances, but her response to the obstacle of paralysis has revealed the glory and fullness of God's light. She realizes that God uses these impediments for His purposes in our lives: "He considers these awful—and often evil—things tragedies, and He takes no delight in misery. But He is de-termined to steer them and use suffering for His own ends."[3]

Today, Joni's outreach to others brings light and life to many suffering people. Among the many things she does for others are the wheelchair teams she sends to underserved areas around the world to construct customized wheelchairs for individuals with disabilities. With all the good that Joni does, it is as though she leaves streaks of colored light across the globe, light that has passed through the prism of her life to reveal the spectrum of God's glory.

— • —

Refraction also causes light to bend a certain way to create what we know as mirages. You may remember a movie or television scene of some helpless soul dragging himself through the parched desert to an apparent nearby oasis, only to find scorching sand where it appeared there was water. What he really saw was refracted light. Many of us have seen a mirage appear on a lonely road on a hot sunny day. The asphalt has absorbed the sun's energy and becomes quite hot. When these conditions exist, the air closest to the surface is hottest and least dense, and the air density gradually increases with height. We actually are viewing light refracted from the sky, but our brains interpret this as water on the road, because water would reflect light from the sky in much the same way that this mirage or "vertical temperature gradient" does.

While there is nothing inherently wrong with this optical illusion, we must be sure to guard against allowing our light to be refracted in such a way that we present a mirage instead of the reality of God.

In addition to the optical illusion that we described, a mirage is also defined as something that's illusory, without substance or reality. Some seem to receive the light from above, but instead of transmitting that light to its fullest, they create an ephemeral image of God. Others may be drawn to this image, like a man dying of thirst in the desert is enticed, but when they find their mouths full of spiritual sand, they feel duped and deluded. They may go through life with a negative image of God because they were introduced to something artificial instead of to the true God who never deceives.

— • —

As Thomas Watson observed, "The curious workmanship of heaven sets forth the glory of its Maker; the firmament is beautified and penciled out in blue and azure colours, where the power and wisdom of God may be clearly seen."[4] Watson understood the power of the light of God. When that light is bent or refracted, it can produce a fleeting mirage, but it also can produce a rainbow of magnificent colors. Bent light, like a bent life, must slow down and change its trajectory—but that change can reveal a newfound power of the light of God, a light that we can then transmit in all its glory.

Will you join me in being a glory-refracting prism, not a mirage that reflects a false picture void of substance?

Signs of Christian Maturity

In all these things we are more than conquerors through
him who loved us.—Romans 8:37

You are growing up in Christ . . .

When circumstances do not affect your peace and joy, but your peace and joy affect your circumstances.

When you learn to dance in the desert and sing in the storm.

When what God says about you is more important than what people say about you.

When character is more important than reputation.

When actions speak louder than words.

When you learn that what you can't shake off, God washes off.

When you believe like Abraham, walk like Enoch, conquer like Joshua, pray like Daniel, touch like Esther, shout like Bartimaeus, climb like Zacchaeus, shine like Stephen, and live like Jesus!

If you have gone through what you have never been through before, it's because you are about to receive what you've never had before.

Unprecedented obstacles . . .

Unprecedented opportunities.

Why Is the Sky Blue?

There is a difference between existing and living.

J ohn Tyndall's father called his young son Newton because of the precocious child's interest in the natural world. While he may not have risen to
his nick-namesake's fame, John Tyndall's experiments laid the groundwork for
answering one of schoolchildren's favorite questions: "Why is the sky blue?"

Because blue skies and all perceived colors are products of light, to Be Light
to our world, we must understand that we will be perceived differently based
on a number of factors, just as light and color are complex and deeply shaped
by perception.

On day eight of this journey of learning more about Being Light, we will
consider the parallels between the sun's white light and the light of God. Sunlight is perceived as yellow, red, blue, and other colors basically because of impurities in our atmosphere that the light travels through and our eyes see. In a
similar fashion, God's pure light shines into the "atmosphere" of our lives and
reveals the impurities within us.

The interaction of light with matter contributes to the appearance of color
in our surrounding world. The ability of the human eye to distinguish colors
is based upon the varying sensitivity of different cells in the retina to light of
different wavelengths. The exact nature of color perception, and indeed the

status of color as a feature of our perception of the world, is a matter of complex and continuing philosophical dispute. Light, no matter how complex its composition of wavelengths, is reduced to three color components by the human eye.

Color-sensing cones or color-receptive cells in our retinas help us perceive color. While most humans are "trichromatic" (having three types of color receptors), many animals, known as "tetrachromats," have four types. These include some species of spiders, most marsupials, birds, reptiles, and many species of fish. And as many as half of all women, but only a small percentage of men, are retinal tetrachromats. (This fact is unsurprising!)

The sky's color, whether blue, yellow, red, or brilliant white is a product of a number of factors. Primary among them is particulate matter in the atmosphere called aerosols, which are tiny suspended particles. These aerosols come from a number of sources, some natural and some not, and can be solid, liquid, or a mixture of both. What John Tyndall discovered was that he could shine a light into a glass tube that was filled with a mixture of chemicals that produced very fine particles suspended in the solution. These particles were uniform in size, and as the light reflected off of them, they produced a blue hue that Tyndall described as rivaling the "deepest and bluest Italian sky."

Tyndall immediately connected his experiment to our perception of the sky's color. He realized that as white light (made up of the full color spectrum) from the sun passes through our atmosphere, the high frequencies (blue, indigo, and violet) become scattered by atmospheric particles, and the lower frequencies (red, orange, and yellow) most likely pass through the atmosphere without significant alteration in their direction. This scattering of the higher frequencies of light illuminates the skies with light on the blue, indigo, and violet end of the visible spectrum. Though violet light is most easily scattered by atmospheric particles, our eyes are more sensitive to light with blue frequencies. Thus, we view the skies as being blue.[1]

One of the features of the light of God is that it reveals our shortcomings.

Just as sunlight reveals particles in the atmosphere, God's light exposes the "pollution" in our lives. Professor W. F. Adeney reminds us, "We never know how odious our sin is till we look at it in God's light. Hidden and forgotten sin is not repented of. Pride grows on the graves of buried sins."[2]

As difficult as it is to have our sins revealed by God's light, His light is meant to bring us to a new awareness of our shortcomings, as we work diligently to cleanse ourselves of unrighteous thoughts and acts that separate us from God.

The purpose of God is greater than the brokenness of man. God is more interested in changing your heart than your circumstances. Change begins in the heart.

— • —

One of the foundational facts of this book and our thirty days together is that God is light. And God's Word tells us, "If we walk in the light, as he is in the light, we have fellowship with one another, and the blood of Jesus, his Son, purifies us from all sin" (1 John 1:7). It is as though God's light goes beyond just revealing our failures; it also brings healing to our hurting lives.

Dallas Willard said, "Almost all evil deeds and intents are begun with the thought that *they can be hidden* by deceit."[3] We must never forget that God's light will find our hidden sin and reveal it, which challenges us to deal with those things in our lives that pollute our relationship with Him and with one another. In some ways, we can say that the atmosphere's color could be rated based on the impurities in it. At a very basic level, we could represent it like this:

Bright white and yellow light	Purest atmosphere
Blue and violet light	Some particulates or impurities
Orange and red light	Many impurities

We could use a similar color scale for our own lives as we consider how we are letting God's pure light reveal what is inside each of us:

Closest to God	Few "impurities" in our lives; sin doesn't hold us captive
Feeling a bit separate from God	Sin has begun to fill our lives
Feeling far from God	Our lives are like a "red sky at morning" because of sin

Just as our eyes have developed receptors to perceive blue light, our spirits have to be developed to perceive God's place and presence around us. The most basic level of enlightenment is the knowledge of sin. Psalm 18:28 says, "You, O LORD, keep my lamp burning; my God turns my darkness into light." This reference makes it clear that God can cleanse us from wrongdoing just as the rain cleanses the atmosphere.

A later psalm says, "The unfolding of your words gives light; it gives understanding to the simple" (119:130). This verse establishes the basic method of God's illumination: when God's Word enters a person's heart, it gives light and understanding.

John Tyndall carried out hundreds of experiments with light as he realized how particles suspended in gas would create different colors. While we spent our first week focusing on reflecting, absorbing, and emitting light as people called to Be Light, we begin week two thinking about how God's light can diffuse when it strikes us. If there is sin—hidden or not—in our lives, the pure light of God will be clouded, and we will not be effective in our calling to Be Light.

Like me you may have boarded a plane on a dreary day and taken off into a gloom that cloaks the sky. Then, as the plane rises through the clouds, pure light pours through the window and the clouds instantly disappear. So is it a cloudy day or a clear one? It depends on your altitude and perspective. That is the way with light. That is the way with color.

The next time a young voice asks, "Why is the sky blue?" one way to answer is to say the sky isn't really blue at all. It only appears blue, and that will change, depending on things like the time of day and the position of the sun. But one thing will not change about the sky. All its light and all its color are products of the sun, which reveals details about the atmosphere that surrounds us.

So it is with our God. If we allow His light to beam into our lives, revealing both the good and bad, He promises to uncover colors in us we have never known.

The Process of Grace

He himself bore our sins in his body on the tree, so that we might die to sins and live for righteousness.—1 Peter 2:24

Photosynthesis is the process by which a tree or plant takes in carbon dioxide and the residual waste from the environment and, with the energy from the sun, converts and purifies that waste into oxygen.

Jesus operates like that. He takes in our sins, our filth, and our spiritual waste and, through a process the Bible calls grace, produces the breath of life.

Give God all your waste! God will release fresh spiritual oxygen into your life. *Breathe!*

Burn Bright

What you can't shake off, Jesus washes off!

In 1880 Wilhelm Wien's parents reluctantly pulled their young son out of school and brought him home to work on the family farm. Though they had hoped Wilhelm would have an academic career, his instructors complained that Wilhelm would often wander into the fields surrounding the school and was unprepared for his mathematics courses.

Few would have guessed that this same young man would go on to win the Nobel Prize in physics after such an undistinguished start. While many other scientists who made discoveries about light dazzled instructors with their prodigious intellect, Wilhelm was a shy man, an academic late bloomer who would ultimately conduct the research that laid the groundwork for quantum physics.

Among Wien's accomplishments was his work on radiation, which led to the establishment of what is now known as Wien's law. Simply stated, the law says that hotter objects emit their radiation at shorter wavelengths and appear bluer. Cooler objects have longer wavelengths and appear redder (so the phrase "red hot" perhaps should be "blue hot"). In addition, Wien's law states that hotter objects—at any wavelength—radiate more and are more luminous than cooler ones.

As we continue to live into the ideal that we are the light of the world, we must apply the simple principle that Wien discovered and shine intensely, burn hot, and be luminous.

In her song "Burn Bright," vocalist Natalie Grant offers these words:

Child of everlasting light
Made to blaze away the night[1]

We are looking deeply into the qualities of natural light in order to find deeper spiritual understanding of how we as "children of everlasting light" can blaze in life as we reflect God's light and love.

Today's principle is as basic as it is profound: we need a sustaining, intense light to burn within us if we are to fulfill our destiny. Teacher and theologian Charles Spurgeon often said that if we want to truly reach others with a transforming power, there are five things we must have: "*light, fire, faith, life, love.* Their number is five, so you may count them on your fingers; their value is inestimable, so grasp them with firm hand, and let them be carried in your hearts."[2] Spurgeon understood the critical interrelationship between these five; in truth, they are inseparable. He argued that God's light is reflected in us as we let the light of knowledge, the power of joy, and the gleaming beauty of truth shine through us. He knew that darkness always threatens to break into our lives, but he reminded us that those who believe the doctrines of grace and have the bearings of God's truth will know what and where they are. And they will not be deceived by the prince of darkness!

We all know that a fire that burns hot can quickly flame out, but perhaps that awareness has kept us from burning as brightly as we should. So often I hear people say, "A little faith is better than none at all," and "I am not the best person, but I am not the worst either!" For these thirty days together, we are determined to refine our light and have it burn as hot and long and clear and bright as possible. We may say that we do not want to be fanatics, but we certainly don't want to be spiritually apathetic either. Here again Spurgeon's words hit the mark: "Even fanaticism is to be preferred to indifference. I had sooner risk the dangers of a tornado of religious excitement than see the air grow stagnant with a dead formality. It is far better for people to be too hot than to be lukewarm." Intense light is never cold. "No fire is moderately hot."[3] Spurgeon imagined an angel with a giant thermometer taking the temperature of every church and every congregant to determine their spiritual temperature.

I don't believe we want to wait another day to burn brighter. Let's now raise our temperature and share the light of God with others!

— • —

I recently read an amazing story about a young woman who encountered the transforming light of God in the midst of the darkest situation:

> As a child I struggled with being a good kid, and from there I endured pain that no child should have ever endured. I was child abused at the age of 6, molested by a family member whom I thought I could trust, and from there I was taken away from my parents for 4 years by the child protective services.
>
> I was returned to my parents 4 years later. I was different; I learned a lot but still didn't know God. I was still lost and searching, so as years passed by I knew I needed Him [but] just couldn't understand why I was compelled to follow Him.
>
> But at the age of 18 I was gang raped by one of my cousin's boyfriends and his friends. . . . On top of all that I became homeless at 18. I had nowhere to stay because my mom had put me out when she found out that I was pregnant.
>
> I struggled to accept that God was real or that [He] even cared about me. So I kind of drifted through life until one day, I was at my lowest and I asked God, "If you truly love me, care so much about me then please save me from myself." . . . [A]t the time I was asking God this very crucial request I was in the midst of committing suicide

because I felt that was all I ever deserved (heart-ache, disappointment, abuse, neglect). But God had a better plan for me and as time passed I learned to forgive others for what they had done to me.

I learned that God just wanted what was best for me. Now, today, after 5 years I've been drug free, and have had no suicide attempts, but I still struggle with accepting myself. And I'm a Christian, have been for almost 5 1/2 years and still have a long way to go. God is so awesome. He can change anyone's circumstances but we have to believe and have faith that God will come through for us in our good and our bad moments. Even when everything seems to be dark and there seems to be no light, remember that Christ is the light and that we must hold on to God's Word.[4]

Holding on to God requires letting go of self.

How the light of God—the light that saved this precious woman—must shine through her today despite her struggles. An old Irish blessing for a time of sorrow says, "May you see God's light on the path ahead when the road you walk is dark." It sounds like that is precisely what this woman experienced.

When we just glance at the brightest, hottest objects like the sun or a pure beam of light, we can close our eyes and the bright image remains. If we commit to seeking God above all things, He will transform us into objects that glow so hot and bright that after others encounter us and walk away, the "bright image" of God's love will remain with them. How would we like to be seen by others? What descriptors would we prefer they use? I can't imagine too many of us getting upset if we were referred to as luminous.

Presence=Power!

But you will receive power when the Holy Spirit comes upon you. And you will be my witnesses, telling people about me everywhere—in Jerusalem, throughout Judea, in Samaria, and to the ends of the earth.—Acts 1:8, NLT

People of light are people of power! If God's presence fills your life, then you have power:

Power to cast out whatever is not right.

Power to move whatever stands in your way.

Power to walk in the midst of storms.

Power to speak truth with love.

Power to shake off the dust.

Power to preach the Word.

Power to walk in holiness.

Power to do justice.

Power to love mercy.

Power to say yes.

Power to say no.

Power to shine the light.

Power to change the world!

LASER-Focused for the Lord

God does not call the perfect;
He calls the willing.

I n 1957 a graduate student at Columbia University named Gordon Gould had been working with "pumping" atoms to higher energy states so they would emit light. As Gould elaborated his ideas and speculated about all the things that could be done with a concentrated beam of light, he realized he was onto something. In his notebook he confidently named the yet-to-be-invented device a LASER (for Light Amplification by Stimulated Emission of Radiation).

Nearly sixty years later, we are still seeing the impact of this remarkable tool. Very recently, Lockheed Martin boasted about their new laser, a ground-based prototype system that burned through an entire car engine in seconds. From a mile away. The company called this laser system the most "efficient and lethal" version on the planet.[1]

As we come to the tenth leg of our journey together, we will focus on the laser, perhaps the most powerful expression of light on earth.

From a spiritual perspective the laser represents the ultimate expression of the impact we can have in a world in need of light. If we are able to understand the stunning power of unity expressed in a laser beam and translate it into our own lives, we might have a greater impact on those around us than ever before.

— • —

A laser is a device that projects a highly concentrated, narrow beam of light that is amplified to great brightness using stimulated radiation. Laser light is very different from normal light. Laser light has the following properties:

- The light released is monochromatic. It contains one specific wavelength of light (one specific color).
- The light released is coherent. It is "organized"—each photon moves in step with the others. This means that all the photons have wave fronts that launch in unison.
- The light is directional. A laser light has a very tight beam and is strong and concentrated.

To make these three properties occur takes something called stimulated emission. In stimulated emission, photon emission is remarkably organized.

Simply expressed, the photon that any atom releases has a certain wavelength (don't we all!). If this photon encounters another atom that has an electron in the same excited state, stimulated emission can occur. The first photon can stimulate atomic emission such that the photon from the second atom vibrates with the same frequency and direction.

The other key to a laser is a pair of mirrors, one at each end of the lasing medium. Photons, with a very specific wavelength and phase, reflect off the mirrors to travel back and forth through the lasing medium. A cascade effect occurs, and soon we have many, many photons of the same wavelength. The special mirror at one end of the laser reflects some light and lets some light through. The light that makes it through is the laser light.

This description of a laser brings together many of the attributes of light we have been studying. For instance, we see that lasers take advantage of the reflective power of mirrors. But the difference between laser light and the light we have been studying is also strikingly different, and that difference is primarily based on one thing: *unity.* Because the photons are of the same wavelength, the light is coherent, directional, and seems to be in unison. We have all seen laser light shows, or perhaps have held a small laser device, and marveled at the tight beam and remarkable power.

— • —

If we are to be the light of the world, what can we emulate regarding the unity displayed by a laser that gives it such power? The first parallel that comes to mind relates to the fact that laser light is all "on the same wavelength." To develop laser light qualities, we must begin by unifying our hearts, minds, and lives to God. If we can find true unity with Him, we will begin to see the power like that of the laser light in our lives.

God created us in His image, and He is light, so we bear that same imprint. If we can get on God's wavelength, we will surely experience the coherence and direction that a laser has. Aligning our light's wavelength with the Lord's is predicated on our desire to be like Him. We must develop a redemptive view of the world around us, pouring out mercy to others, bringing grace to those in need, and denying ourselves. We must hate sin the way God does, knowing that sin always keeps us from being on the same wavelength as God. Being one with the Lord and joining Him in the pure light of salvation requires everything from us: we are one with Him when we are hidden in Him, away from the darkness of sin and selfishness.

One of the astonishing features that differentiates laser light from normal light is the way the photon of laser light can stimulate a second atom so that it vibrates with the same frequency and direction.

As Christ followers we are called to encounter others around us—like this "excited" photon—and stimulate them to release their light. But we are not encouraging others to simply release their own wavelength of light but to match our own—and vice versa. In doing so, we are agreeing that the light that is coming from the two of us, when aligned perfectly so that the length and color are exactly the same, becomes transformed into a laser for God's purposes. Others are drawn to this light and are compelled to produce a light that matches the intensity of the unified light. This is not a light that reduces us to sameness, but rather it elevates us to the very nature of God, whose intense light illuminates all truth and life.

The Bible is filled with examples of the power that comes when people unify in faith. When mankind built the Tower of Babel, the Lord said, "Behold, they are one people, and they have all one language, and this is only the beginning of what they will do. And nothing that they propose to do will now be impossible for them" (Genesis 11:6, ESV).

Jesus Himself said that whenever "two of you on earth agree about anything you ask for, it will be done for you by my Father in heaven" (Matthew 18:19). He later prayed, "Holy Father, keep them in your name, which you have given me, that they may be one, even as we are one" (John 17:11, ESV).

It is certain that the light that emanates from us when we are in unity will have a distinct and transcendent power. When God's people unify their light, their identities flow into His, as though God Himself becomes the means by which our light is concentrated and then beamed out to the world. Lasers are used to heal damaged skin, improve hepatitis C, cut away disease, and even switch a mouse's memories from positive to negative. The light God has given us has that same power and more if we direct it so that it can join with others' and produce an impenetrable beam of light to shine through us.

— ● —

We now have a far clearer understanding of the complexity and beauty of light. Light, the substance that we often take for granted, is a gift that brings life and illumination wherever it goes. Light is powerful, fast, healing, and capable of driving darkness away in an instant.

We are the light of the world. We must be intentional and refine the use of our light. We must be sure our light is placed in such a fashion that it is not eclipsed by anything. Our light must shine before all people because our light will reflect the only true and transcendent light, the Creator of light and life, our eternal God.

For the next ten days, we will shift our focus to light's enemy: darkness. We will not delve into its nature for long, but instead suggest that darkness is present—and sometimes feels omnipresent—but it cannot overcome the light within us. Instead, we will overcome darkness, replacing it with the light of God. We have already been empowered to overcome any darkness we face, so we will now shift our attention to how we can live in the freedom of victory over the forces of evil.

The Lord's Sight

The LORD doesn't see things the way you see them. People judge by outward appearance, but the LORD looks at the heart.—1 Samuel 16:7, NLT

The Lord doesn't see things the way you see them!

The Lord has "heart-ray vision."

He is not nearsighted or farsighted.

He doesn't suffer from glaucoma.

He doesn't see what we see.

We see dirt; He sees clay.

We see a crushed grape; He sees new wine.

We see a murderer; He sees a liberator.

We see a liar; He sees the father of faith.

He doesn't see things the way we see them.

We see a drug addict; He sees a pastor.

We see a corrupt politician; He sees a prophet.

We see a young lady fighting with depression; He sees a missionary.

We Must Have Oil for Our Lamps

Doubt amplifies darkness. Fear attracts darkness. Unforgiveness is darkness.

As people called to be the light of the world, we are drawn again to what the Bible says about light and what it might teach us.

One of the most powerful passages in the Bible related to light is one in which Jesus tells a parable—a fictional story with a moral takeaway—about ten bridesmaids who are participating in a wedding. Each of them is asked to take a lamp and meet the bridegroom. Here is the story:

> Then the Kingdom of Heaven will be like ten bridesmaids who took their lamps and went to meet the bridegroom. Five of them were foolish, and five were wise. The five who were foolish didn't take enough olive oil for their lamps, but the other five were wise enough to take along extra oil. When the bridegroom was delayed, they all became drowsy and fell asleep.
>
> At midnight they were roused by the shout, "Look, the bridegroom is coming! Come out and meet him!"
>
> All the bridesmaids got up and prepared their lamps. Then the five foolish ones asked the others, "Please give us some of your oil because our lamps are going out."

But the others replied, "We don't have enough for all of us. Go to a shop and buy some for yourselves."

But while they were gone to buy oil, the bridegroom came. Then those who were ready went in with him to the marriage feast, and the door was locked. Later, when the other five bridesmaids returned, they stood outside, calling, "Lord! Lord! Open the door for us!"

But he called back, "Believe me, I don't know you!"

So you, too, must keep watch! For you do not know the day or hour of my return. (Matthew 25:1–13, NLT)

The story reveals a number of ancient Hebrew wedding practices. It was typical for the bridegroom himself to go in person—and often at night—to bring his new bride to his home for the wedding festivities about to take place there. Before leaving the house that had been her home, she would receive the blessing of her relatives, and there would often be a procession from her childhood home to her future home. Jesus seems to be making reference to these ancient practices, as the bridesmaids are all awaiting the groom and need to be ready for his arrival. In fact the groom would often not give a specific time for his arrival so that he would heighten the bride's expectation of his coming.

In describing a first-century Jewish wedding, D. A. Carson, in *The Expositor's Bible Commentary,* explained the setting for the story this way:

Normally the bridegroom with some close friends left his home to go to the bride's home, where there were various ceremonies, followed by a procession through the streets—after nightfall—to his home. The ten virgins may be bridesmaids who have been assisting the bride; they expect to meet the groom as he comes from the bride's house. . . . Everyone in the procession was expected to carry his or her own torch. Those without a torch would be assumed to be party crashers or even brigands. The festivities, which might last several days, would formally get under way at the groom's house.[1]

Our focus turns to the light in the story and what we might learn from it. It is clear that each person meeting the groom (Jesus) is required to have and be responsible for her own lamp. It is also clear that it is not enough to just have a lamp; she must have enough fuel—olive oil in this case—to keep it burning brightly. The original word used for the bridesmaids' lights, *lampas,* is closer to the word we use for *torch.* In Jesus's day these were probably little more than a rag soaked in oil sitting in a curved ceramic bowl. The bowl would have to be periodically filled with olive oil, so that is why there is a reference to extra oil in the story. Each bridesmaid should have carried a flask of some kind with reserve oil in it.

There are many applications from this story to help us better understand our calling to Be Light. We want to be like the five bridesmaids who were wise enough to bring extra oil. This planning reflects that we realize that our light, by nature, will get dim and burn out. We read that the five foolish bridesmaids had enough oil to get their torches lit but then soon after realized their torches were "going out." The light of joy, of salvation, of truth is always subject to diminishment. We must actively prepare for this to occur and "carry oil" to sustain us on the dark days when our light—like the torches of the five foolish bridesmaids—does not have enough fuel to sustain it.

What is the "oil" we must keep with us each day to be sure our flaming light burns hot? The most critical is God's holy Word. We know it is a "lamp unto [our] feet" (Psalm 119:105, kjv) and a light-sustaining, irreplaceable power source for our souls. Each day things come into our lives that can extinguish our light, but God's Word reminds us that His promises never fail and we do not have to fear. His Word tells us the truth so that we can rely on it fully and not trust our own understanding or be shaken by our circumstances.

The oil for our lamps is also the Holy Spirit. Jesus said He was going to heaven so that He could then send us the Comforter, the Holy Spirit, to strengthen us in dark times. In the Old Testament, Zechariah had a dream in which he saw a vision of the golden lampstand that was meant to stand in the temple. In addition to the lampstand, Zechariah saw something that was never before in the temple: two olive trees that supplied the seven lamps with oil through seven pipes.

Zechariah asked, "What are these, my lord?" Zechariah saw the vision but didn't understand what it meant. So God answered and said to him, "This is the word of the LORD . . . : 'Not by might nor by power, but by my Spirit,' says the LORD Almighty" (Zechariah 4:4, 6). God was showing Zechariah—and showing us today—that the Holy Spirit can supply us with the oil we need to keep our lamps burning.

We are the light of the world. Our mission is to pierce the darkness with the light of Christ:

- Christ the Messiah
- Christ the Conqueror
- Christ the Son of Man
- Christ the Son of God
- Christ the Way, the Truth, and the Life
- Christ the Resurrection and the Life
- Christ the true Vine
- Christ the good Shepherd
- Christ the Alpha and the Omega
- Christ the Author and Finisher of our faith, the One who changed water into wine, sinners into saints, and mourning into dancing
- Christ the Hope of Glory

Yet there is one descriptor for Jesus that commands our particular attention. He is not only the Savior, Deliverer, and Healer. Isaiah 54:5 makes our relationship with God clear: "For your Maker is your *husband*—the LORD Almighty is his name—the Holy One of Israel is your Redeemer."

If Christ is the Bridegroom, then what are we as His church? We are not just any other faith narrative, and we are not just a community of believers; *we are His bride.* We are the wise, prepared bridesmaids who may fall asleep, but when the Groom arrives, we will have enough oil to light torches of purity and truth to light the wedding procession from this dark world to His world of light and life.

God is getting us ready for the eternal wedding! He is the Bridegroom and we are His bride.

The question is, what is a Bridegroom willing to do for His bride? And what kind of bride is He coming for? He's not coming back for a defeated church, a depressed church, a discouraged church, a divided church.

The Bridegroom is coming for a glorious church, a holy church, a triumphant church, a pure church, a worshiping church, and a shining church.

"Husbands, love your wives, just as Christ loved the church and gave himself up for her to make her holy, cleansing her by the washing with water through the word, and to present her to himself as a radiant church, without stain or wrinkle or any other blemish, but holy and blameless" (Ephesians 5:25–27).

As the bride full of light we preach not to conform but to convert. We preach for the purpose of Acts 26:18: "to open their eyes and turn them from darkness to light, and from the power of Satan to God, so that they may receive forgiveness of sins and a place among those who are sanctified by faith in me."

We must Be Light by saturating the world with the oil in our lamps. In Exodus we read, "Command the people of Israel to bring you pure oil of pressed olives for the light, to keep the lamps burning continually" (27:20, NLT). Continually, from Zechariah's vision to Matthew 25 and the parable of the ten bridesmaids, from the Old to the New Testament, there stands both an exegetical and expository truth worthy of engagement: in order to Be Light we must have oil in our lamps! Let me say that one more time: in order to Be Light, *we must have oil in our lamps!*

In this season, for us and for our country, we do not need more churches. America doesn't need more preachers. America doesn't need more ministries. America needs more churches, more preachers, and more ministries with oil in their lamps.

Be Light by saturating the world with a lamp filled with fresh oil!

Plenty of Oil!

Wake up, O sleeper,

    rise from the dead,

and Christ will shine on you.—Ephesians 5:14

Today, we stand renewed. Today and tomorrow, we will . . .

Be Light by saturating the world as the wise bride.

Be Light by saturating the world with fresh oil in our lamps!

Be Light by saturating the world with a fresh anointing! Be anointed.

Be Light by saturating the world with purity!

Without the anointing we toil in the world of the pathetic. With the anointing we soar in the land of the prophetic.

Because we believe that the church is the bride of Christ, we realize that part of the message of this story is for each of us, as we await Jesus's return.

We will have our lamps ready.

We will bring extra oil.

We are the light of the world.

Shining Brightly in a World of Brilliance

Surround yourself with people who speak into you and not about you.

One of the most difficult things to envision is the dark world into which Jesus has commanded us to Be the Light of the world. Today, we have an entirely new vocabulary than that of first-century Israel. Now we know about amps, volts, and watts, and some of us are familiar with words like *joules* and *galvanic cells*. But in Jesus's day, night would bring a cloak of darkness that we can almost not imagine. With the sunset came darkness, danger, and fear.

After Abraham made his covenant with God, he fell into a deep sleep, "and a thick and dreadful darkness came over him" (Genesis 15:12), after which God told him his descendants would be enslaved for four hundred years.

Darkness was one of the plagues that God brought to Egypt through Moses. The darkness was so heavy that an Egyptian could physically feel it. All work stopped. Human interaction came to a halt, and even time itself seemed affected.

Such is the power of darkness. Humans need light.

The ancient Greeks were fascinated with light and electricity. They stood with bare feet on electric eels to treat gout. They also realized that amber, the fossilized secretion of plants, when rubbed with a piece of wool, created sparks. They believed this substance had a "soul," and "seemed to live, and exercise an attraction upon other things distant from it."[1] They believed that amber derived from the tears of the Heliades, Phaëthon's sisters who wept so long beside the river where he'd drowned that the gods in their pity turned them into poplars.

But the sparks amber created would not lead to electric light for centuries. Instead, people in Jesus's day relied on far more rudimentary ways to illuminate their lives after dark. The oldest light source was animal fat, but it burned quickly and had a foul odor. In the West Indies, Japan, and other nations, fireflies were caged and used as primitive lights. (Today, artificial light is so bright at night that it makes it difficult for fireflies to attract mates.) Some islanders used oily nuts that burned on the end of sticks, while others dried oily fish like salmon and burned it. But in the Middle East, olive oil was favored, as it was plentiful, odorless, and clean burning.

Today's world is illuminated in such brilliance that night and day are equally bright in many homes, neighborhoods, and cities. As Jane Brox pointed out in her book *Brilliant: The Evolution of Artificial Light,* "On a map of the earth at night as seen from space—made up of a composite of images from satellite photographs taken on nights of the new moon—light blooms across the continents like yeast in warm, sweet water." She went on to say that mountains and deserts are still comparatively dark but that "the most glaring spots on the map correspond to flagrancy and prosperity rather than density of human habitation: at the moment, the eastern seaboard of the United States is brighter than anyplace in China or India. Only parts of the oceans and the poles appear completely dark."[2]

Light is surely taken for granted in today's world, but its pervasiveness has not blunted its impact. Even today a flame will mesmerize us as few other objects do. French philosopher Gaston Bachelard attributed our fascination with fire to humankind's long connection with the incomparable glow that emanates from the tiniest flame: "We are almost certain that fire is precisely the first object, the *first phenomenon,* on which the human mind *reflected.*"[3] Whatever the reason, from campfires in our Boy and Girl Scout youths, to bonfires for a beach celebration, to fireworks on the Fourth of July, we are all enthralled by light.

One reason we are so drawn to light is that it has always brought with it a sense of safeness and even comfort. How many of us turn a light on in a room we are not occupying, just because it makes us feel better? We also switch on porch lights at dusk and leave them on all night—almost as a sign of hospitality to our neighbors and others. Many history books recount that even in the Middle Ages burglars avoided nights with a full moon, and we still believe that bright light is a deterrent to crime (even though the research is mixed regarding this conclusion).

French geologist Michel Siffre descended into the Scarasson Cave in 1962, where he resided in a tent for over two months. He surely felt the comfort and safety light can bring: "When I left the lightbulb on and went outside, the tent glowed in the cold darkness with a redness that was singularly comforting. From the moraine I often looked back at it with a feeling of love. It represented security and shelter."[4]

Despite light's positive effects, some say we now actually have too much light in our world. While "light pollution" is not a phrase that is heard in much of the third world, others have known it for years. Scientists at the Palomar Observatory outside of San Diego, California, have long worked with local businesses and homeowners to reduce the amount of light they use at night so that objects in the night sky are not occluded by the area's night brightness. Fairly recently, astronomers David Crawford and Tim Hunter established the International Dark-Sky Association for "the express purpose of abating light pollution and increasing public awareness of the consequences of excess light." They point out that reducing the use of light could save over one billion dollars in the United States annually and suggest that urban planning should always include how to most efficiently save money and reduce the negative impact of excess light.[5]

— • —

As people of faith instructed to Be Light, we can draw a number of parallels between our lives as Christ followers and the development of light in history. Just as it is true that candles and other illumination were once rare, faith in Christ was once a rarity as well. But with the explosion of communication channels and the diligent work of evangelists and missionaries across the world, the Christian faith has spread like billions of points of light scattered across our globe. According to the statistical tables produced by the respected Center for the Study of Global Christianity, some 2.3 billion Christians were alive in 2010, about one-third of the planetary population. The largest group is still in Europe—some 588 million—but Latin America is not far behind. Africa has seen the most explosive growth, from 8.7 million in 1900 to 542 million today, to perhaps 1.2 billion by 2050—matching the combined total of Europe and Latin America.[6]

Christians today are like fireflies. Once upon a time, a few of us could illuminate an entire city with the light of God shining into the darkness. Today, our light is often muted by the proliferation of professing believers, and the glow of our faith is lost in the midst of a cultural Christianity that is neither brilliant nor exceptional. The searing light of a pure faith has often been replaced by a feeble, lukewarm belief that is hard to distinguish from no faith at all. Without sounding judgmental, I would say the reality is that many who profess faith attend church regularly, may even pray from time to time, curse less, refrain from overindulgences, and are known to be courteous. Yet their core being has not been transformed by the power of God.

Apologist and author Ravi Zacharias, in his book *Why Jesus? Rediscovering His Truth in an Age of Mass Marketed Spirituality,* explained the dilemma of a world where many lights can diminish the true light. He wrote,

> Tired, in the West, of what C. S. Lewis called "the same old thing,"
> and having become accustomed to abundance and the bliss of multiple
> choice, we have now a spiritual supermarket before us from which we

may choose whatever form of spirituality we fancy. We think we can follow whichever path we want and still end up with something meaningful.[7]

Our light is not something that can be rebranded and distributed as the true light of God. We must stand out among the many lights of pretense in our midst and shine the incomparable light of Christ.

— • —

Here on the twelfth segment of our study together, we ask and try to answer the question, How can we still shine brightly in a world where it seems that everyone has heard the gospel and there is so much light that our little beams seem insignificant? For starters, we must fight against compromise that brings disgrace to our Lord and diminishes our impact. We all cringe when we hear coworkers speaking openly about their passionate faith in God, but their personal practices and attitudes do not reflect the excellence and humility to which we are called. We are described as the light of the world, but we should not confuse this description to mean that we turn the spotlight onto ourselves. As this book continues to remind us, we are always reflecting the light and power of God and never want the light to focus on us. We cannot Be Light until we discover who we are. We cannot Be Light until we repudiate any identity moratorium.

In addition to eliminating compromise in our lives, standing out in a world full of religion means that we must shine more brightly. Author and speaker Joyce Meyer put it this way:

Sometimes God places us in situations where we're uncomfortable just so we turn the light up a little bit brighter. To do this, we don't have to get all "religious." There's no need for you to walk around with your six-pack of Bibles and covered head to toe with bumper stickers. All you need to do is let your light shine. Loving, calm, happy, gracious behavior will stand out. That will be a light in a dark place.[8]

I recently attended a Christian conference at a well-known hotel in Washington, DC. At the end of the three-day conference, I was speaking to the guest services agent at checkout. She began this way: "I have been working here for over six years, but I have never . . ." I reflexively thought, *Oh no. Here goes. She is about to tell me how rude we have been over the last seventy-two hours.* Instead, she continued, ". . . ever met such kind, thoughtful people. They all were calm, and even made me feel special—which is what I thought I was supposed to do for them!"

There is no question that we get desensitized to many things that are a part of our daily lives. Few of us ever consider taking time to thank God for the basics—food, water, and shelter—but a grateful life and attitude are hallmarks of a true Christian life committed to God. Yes, many have heard the gospel, and information about our faith saturates airwaves and fills television sets from Bismarck to Birmingham. But some recent statistics say that even with the spread of the gospel, 20 percent of non-Christians in North America today say they don't know even one Christian person![9] The true light of God needs to shine through us now more than ever.

Pastor Ray Stedman put it this way:

If the life your neighbors see in you is explainable only in terms of your human personality and background, what do you have to say to your neighbors that will awaken them to their need of Christ? If the situations you face cause you to react with the same murmuring and discontent and bitterness they have, what's the difference between your quality of life and theirs? They will simply say my life is explained in terms of my personality. I like certain sports and entertainment, and certain kinds of music and you like religion—that's all. Unless there is a quality of life that can be explained only in terms of God there is nothing to challenge the world around.[10]

Challenging the world around us is the only way our light can shine in a world full of religious options, each clamoring for its light to be viewed as the brightest and best. Instead of disputing with our words, we must begin today to look inwardly and ensure that we are doing all we can to stand out for Christ in a world where false light is perhaps more dangerous than darkness. We must realize that just as light pollution from a city makes it impossible to see the stars in the night sky, "religious pollution" from false teaching can produce a false light that will keep others from seeing the truth embodied in the risen Christ.

Be Light by Example

Then [Gideon] said to them, "Keep your eyes on me.

When I come to the edge of the camp, do just as I do."

—Judges 7:17, NLT

Gideon said, "Do what I do. Follow my example."

We, too, must set the example. Why are we imitating the world when the world should be imitating us?

Is your life worthy of imitating? The quintessential metric of a believer is to live a life worthy of imitation.

More than praying to be rich, popular, or even loved, our prayer must be, *Make me a godly example.*

No Lucky Stars, Just God's Heavenly Bodies

I am who I AM says I am.

O n the thirteenth day of our study, it is difficult to focus on how to Be Light with that "unlucky" number thirteen staring back at us. We might be tempted to take a day off and just come back tomorrow, but instead let's illuminate the whole idea of *lucky* and *unlucky* so that our true light can shine as we eliminate ideas like *luckiness* that are so ingrained in our consciousness they can dim even the brightest light.

We have all heard the phrase "thank my lucky stars," but why do we believe that stars are lucky at all? Pop star Madonna had her first top-five hit with her song "Lucky Star," and some of the lyrics to the song would almost have you think she is making reference to God:

And when I'm lost you'll be my guide
I just turn around and you're by my side.[1]

The Lord is certainly by our side and guides us as He chases darkness from our lives, but He is no "lucky star." He is the unchanging true Light that brings life, not luck, to any person who accepts His love. The phrase "thank my lucky stars" reflects the ancient belief in the influence of stars over human destiny and appeared in slightly different form in Ben Jonson's play *Every Man Out of His*

Humour: "I thank my stars. I thank my stars for it."[2] In Shakespeare's *All's Well That Ends Well,* Helena asks that her father's legacy "be sanctified by the luckiest stars in heaven."[3]

In the era in which both Jonson and Shakespeare lived, the belief in the power of the stars to influence human behavior was especially strong. In fact, King Henry VIII employed Nicholas Kratzer as his royal astronomer, and he was both astronomer and astrologer to the monarch. Among his duties were advising the king regarding the birth of his children, favorable days to initiate war, and the like. Henry's successors had similar predilections, and England's most famous astrologer to the monarch followed Kratzer in the role, the Cambridge scholar John Dee.

Dee became astrologer to Mary Tudor and then to Queen Elizabeth. He practiced astrology and horoscopy in Elizabeth's court and even gave advice to captains and navigators who were exploring the new world. It is said that Elizabeth, like her half sister and father before her, would consult with Dee while planning each day and that he was perhaps her most trusted adviser. So entrenched was the relationship between astrology and religion that it wasn't long before Dee's teaching strayed far from orthodox faith.

So it is with light. Unless we are diligent, it can easily be replaced by a pale reflection.

It is no surprise that the pale yellow star on the right shoulder of the astrological constellation Aquarius is named Sadalmelik, from the Arabic *Al Sa'd al Malik,* the "Lucky One of the King," sometimes expressed as *Al Sa'd al Mulk,* the "Lucky One of the Kingdom." This star and the nearby Sadalsuud, whose name means "Luckiest of the Lucky," is reputed to have been so named because of the weather conditions that accompanied its rising. Latin astrologers knew it by the title *Fortuna Fortunarum,* clear indication of its purported benevolent nature.

It is clear that these stars and related astrological signs are vestiges of pagan beliefs that we must discard completely if we are to shine in the truth that God brings.

As the light of the world, we must shine our light on the emptiness of these ancient false beliefs.

An antiquated system of associating celestial omens with events on the earth began in Mesopotamia after 600 BC, in the centuries "between testaments." This system was eventually adopted by the ancient Greeks following the conquest of Babylonia by Alexander the Great. The version of astrology commonly seen today is based on the failed, discredited pseudoscience of the ancient Greeks.

Astrology has nothing to offer to people interested in truth. Knowing your sign is the equivalent of knowing the shape of purple—both are nonsense. There are no lucky stars. In fact, for people of faith, there is no luck at all.

From tossing pennies into fountains with a passionate whispered wish to breaking glass at weddings, our lives are filled with lingering images of our deep belief in "good fortune." Mathematician Joseph Mazur, in his book *What's Luck Got to Do with It?*, traced the history of gambling from the earliest known evidence of dice playing among Neolithic peoples to the first games of chance during the Renaissance, from government-administered lotteries to the glittering seductions of grand casinos. He eloquently described the psychological and emotional factors that entice people to put their faith in winning that ever-elusive jackpot, despite its mathematical improbability. It is that drive for the unexpected pot of gold—whether material gain or the luck that helps us meet just the right person, avoid an accident, or land the right job—that entices us to create a view of life that includes a place for luck.

A standard definition of the word reveals that *luck* is the force that seems to operate for good or ill in a person's life, as in shaping circumstances, events, or opportunities. Put bluntly, there is no such force, and there is danger in believing that randomness is an inherent part of the universe. A simple, seemingly innocent phrase like "I thank my lucky stars" can reveal a deeper belief about the nature of life.

As people of faith, we are uncompromising in our fundamental belief that there is purpose and design in life's every moment. Shakespeare's Hamlet remarked, "There's a special providence in the fall of a sparrow,"[4] and he was echoing a famous quote from Jesus: "Are not five sparrows sold for two pennies? Yet not one of them is forgotten by God" (Luke 12:6).

Our God is intentional about every action; no one, nothing is forgotten by Him, and to allow chance, luck, and superstition to creep into our worldview is to insult our God of supreme reason and intent.

There is a reason the word *luck* does not appear in the Bible: luck has no place in this world or our view of it.

Be strong and brave. Be Light. Be filled. Be holy. Be still and know that God is in control.

— • —

We are the light of the world; we are not anyone or anything's "lucky stars." In fact we stand as a steady beam of truth against the random world of stargazing, fortune mongering, and chance. There is either divine order or there is not.

As Francis Schaeffer said, "The conclusion that we are the natural products of the impersonal, plus time and chance, is the only one, unless we begin with personality. And no one has shown how time plus chance can produce a qualitative change from impersonal to personal."[5] No one has demonstrated how we have become such personal creatures who believe in a personal God.

The only satisfying answer is that God created us with a longing to know Him and be known by Him. There is no room for chance in a world where God created us, chose us to be His people, then died and rose again to prepare a specific, personal place for each of us.

A. W. Tozer put it this way: "Religion, so far as it is genuine, is in essence the response of created personalities to the Creating Personality, God."[6]

That is our world, a world where a creating God made us to serve Him and love Him as our Father, and that is why we are called to Be Light in it.

Now, that is truly good fortune!

In God We Trust?

Believe in the light while you have the light, so that you may become children of light.—John 12:36, NIV 2011

It's not a matter of understanding; it's a matter of trust.

God is less interested in you understanding Him and more interested in you trusting Him.

So do you really trust Him?

Samuel's mom, Hannah, trusted Him so much she left Samuel at the temple for the Lord (1 Samuel 1).

Here's the word for you today: do likewise. Stop trying to save it, heal it, fix it yourself. Leave it for the Lord.

If you give it to God, He will save it. Our God is a God who saves (Psalm 68:20).

If you give it to God, He will heal it. Our God is a God who heals (Exodus 15:26).

If you give it to God, He will anoint it. Our God anoints (1 John 2:27).

If you give it to God, He will protect it (2 Thessalonians 3:3).

If you give it to God, He will provide for it (Philippians 4:19).

Trust God today!

When the Jar Breaks, Our Lamps Will Shine

God does great things with broken pieces!

I am not sure the first time I heard my wife refer to a hurricane lamp, but I know we have quite a few of them in our home. They are sometimes called a hurricane globe or hurricane shade, with the lamp being the entire fixture and the globe or shade a glass chimney or shield placed over a candle or other light source to keep it from being blown out by the wind. Originally they were made of clear glass but soon became decorative, functioning less as a light source and more as ornamentation.

On day fourteen of this adventure we will focus on letting our light shine before all as we try to Be Light in this world. It would be easy for us to try to protect our light from the "winds" of conflict, change, or a myriad of other things, and we could cover it with a globe or shade. Yet the globe—originally intended to protect our light—could easily become a barrier. Just as hurricane lamps became less utilitarian and more decorative, we must be careful not to let the trappings of religion dim our light from shining brightly.

Many people of faith become entrenched in "doing faith" through Bible studies, attending church, or reading Christian books and forget about "living faith" so that they shine for God.

We read in the Old Testament the remarkable story of Gideon, who before a battle prepared and gave each of his warriors a very unusual weapon: a hurricane lamp. Seriously! Here is the text: "He divided the 300 men into three groups and gave each man a ram's horn and a clay jar with a torch in it" (Judges 7:16, NLT).

Sounds like a version of a hurricane lamp to me, and certainly a nontraditional weapon to say the least. Before we review the details of this incident, here is a brief summary of the events that led up to Gideon distributing the clay jars containing torches.

Israel had been brutally oppressed by the neighboring Midianites for seven years when they cried out to God in desperation. God responded by sending an angel to a young man named Gideon, who was threshing wheat in a winepress. The angel said to Gideon, "The LORD is with you, mighty warrior" (6:12). God told Gideon to lead the Israelites against Midian in battle, but before Gideon responded, God said, "You have too many men. I cannot deliver Midian into their hands, or Israel would boast against me, 'My own strength has saved me'" (7:2, NIV 2011). So the Lord reduced Gideon's army from 32,000 to three hundred, and it is to those three hundred that Gideon gave a ram's horn and a clay jar with a torch inside. Gideon asked the men to follow his lead and smash their clay jars at just the right moment, suddenly revealing the dazzling torchlight, which threw the Midianites into a confused frenzy. This tiny band of strangely equipped warriors then defeated the Midianites, all to the glory of God. While it is difficult to know fully, it seems Gideon's men were so successful because their weapons were so unconventional.

The Bible unites Gideon's story with another passage that uses the image of clay jars. In his second letter to the Corinthian church, Paul wrote, "We now have this light shining in our hearts, but we ourselves are like fragile clay jars containing this great treasure. This makes it clear that our great power is from God, not from ourselves" (4:7, NLT). Just as in Gideon's story, the "great power" will come from God and not from us. We are called "fragile clay jars," but in the hands of a powerful God, we are weapons for victory against tremendous Midian-sized odds.

Are we not God's jars of clay that He—as the everlasting Potter—will smash at just the right moment to reveal His blinding light through us? Are we not the most unconventional weapons of glory that God can use, if we will only surrender to Him?

Just as in Gideon's story, we are both the jar and the light, and God is the Potter: "And yet, O LORD, you are our Father. We are the clay, and you are the potter. We all are formed by your hand" (Isaiah 64:8, NLT).

Here is another passage that further confirms God as the Potter. The Lord said, "'Go down to the potter's house, and there I will give you my message.' So I went down to the potter's house, and I saw him working at the wheel. But the pot he was shaping from the clay was marred in his hands; so the potter formed it into another pot, shaping it as seemed best to him" (Jeremiah 18:2–4).

God was Jeremiah's Potter, and He is still the Potter. He's still committed to molding you in His image. He's still driven to make you right. Why? Because He loves you too much to leave you in any state that's less than glorious. *That's not who you are!*

You are not defined by what people say about you, but by what Jesus did for you.

You are not defined by your failures, but rather by His forgiveness.

You are not defined by what surrounds you, but rather by He who lives inside of you.

When sin, failure, defeat, and discouragement attempt to falsely, narrowly define you, rise up and say, "That's not who I am!"

Instead, say, "He is the Potter and I am the clay. He's molding me, forming me, shaping me in His image, to His specifications. So if I hear a crushing noise, I won't call 911! Rather, I will put on dancing shoes because it means only one thing: the Potter is working in me to make me right! He is my Potter and I am His clay!"

— • —

Don't resist His changes.

Remember Jeremiah 18. The jar he was making did not turn out as he had hoped, so he crushed it into a lump of clay again and started over.

God will do the same for you. When He sees you as less than what He purposed you for, when He sees a jar that does not appear as intended, He has no problem in crushing you and starting over. There's something powerful about starting over! This is a season of starting over. What the devil said is completely over and finished, God says, "Wrong! I am just starting over."

There's a difference between *over* and *starting over*!

I used to play a game called Need for Speed with my son. He would get upset because whenever I was about to lose the game I would "accidentally" press the Start Over button.

God would rather start you over than let you lose! If He sees you are about to fail, He would rather have you start over.

He is the Potter and you are the clay jar.

I dare you to say, *Lord, You are the Potter; I am Your clay jar. Before You place the light, the torch in my life, make my jar just right.*

Gideon led by example: "Then he said to them, 'Keep your eyes on me. When I come to the edge of the camp, do just as I do'" (Judges 7:17, NLT).

We are called to Be Light in the darkest hour. In Gideon's story, the men blew their horns and broke their clay jars, then "Gideon and the hundred men with him reached the edge of the camp at the beginning of the middle watch, just after they had changed the guard" (verse 19). In the midst of great darkness our light will shine brightest! As the Bible says, "The light shines in the darkness, but the darkness has not understood it" (John 1:5). And again, "The night is nearly over; the day is almost here. So let us put aside the deeds of darkness and put on the armor of light" (Romans 13:12).

Another lesson emerges from Gideon's remarkable story. When the jars break, the light will shine. Brokenness exposes the light! In other words, when the flesh is crucified, the spirit thrives. When the Lord truly breaks our wills, our lives—like Gideon's clay jars—are smashed and His torch-bright light is revealed. Nothing shines the light of God like a life broken and redeemed by a loving God.

— • —

Be Light, and your enemies will take care of themselves. In Gideon's story, each of his men held his position around the camp and watched as all the Midianites rushed around in a panic, shouting as they ran to escape. When the three hundred Israelites blew their horns, the Lord caused the warriors in the camp to fight against each other with their swords. Those who were not killed fled.

In the same way, if we embody the light that God has given us, our enemies will scatter like chaff in the wind. Gideon discovered that the Enemy declares war right before the big promotion. If you are in the midst of a fight, rejoice! Your promotion is coming next!

The Red Sea opened, the children of God crossed, and the Egyptians who followed them all drowned . . . *not one survived.* The Enemy will always be defeated in your breakthrough; he can't step into the area God has opened for you.

Gideon was transformed because of the power of God. He was even given the name Jerub-Baal, as one who would fight against the pagan god Baal, who had replaced the everlasting and true God in Gideon's community. Gideon himself rose up and destroyed the pagan altars erected to Baal. He fought the mighty Midianites and won because the Lord whispered these simple words to him: "I will be with you."

God says the same to us today. He may have placed a hurricane shade of clay over us, but it is time to smash the things that cover our light and let our torches shine. They will confuse our enemies and bring new light into the world.

The Bigger They Are . . .

I can do all things through Christ who strengthens me.

—Philippians 4:13, NKJV

Goliath was known for his height; he was approximately nine feet tall. Height matters!

There comes a time in your life when an intimidating, overbearing, behemoth, mammoth, mucho-grande giant shows up. It comes in the way of a problem, bad news, a disease, financial calamity, marital strife, temptation, sin. However it shows up, it represents the biggest challenge of your life.

The size of your giant is directly proportional to the size of your blessing. If the problem is big, it's because the Enemy doesn't want you to see the glory on the other side. Goliath wants to obstruct the view.

You need to understand that for every Goliath there must be a David. Goliath had the height, but David had something Goliath did not. In 1 Samuel 16:13, David received something greater than height, greater than armor. David received *the anointing*!

You may not have the height, may not be as educated, may not have all the money. But there is something you do have: *the anointing*!

What God placed upon you is greater than that which stands before you.

You don't need Saul's armor when you carry God's anointing!

Pick up your sling: your giant is going down!

No Half-Life

There is no such thing as comfortable Christianity.

Ernest Rutherford's first name was mistakenly spelled "Earnest," when his birth was registered in the tiny burg of Brightwater, New Zealand. His father, James, had moved to the island to "raise a little flax and a lot of children."[1] Little did he know that his precocious son was more "earnest" than anyone could have predicted: he went on to be knighted, win a Nobel Prize, and he is called to this day "the father of nuclear physics."

Among his achievements was the discovery of the principle of a *half-life period,* which has been shortened to *half-life.* Today we hear the term most in reference to nuclear waste and how to safely deal with decaying nuclear materials. Rutherford used the measurement to determine the age of rocks, but the term is now used generically to describe any period of time in which a quantity falls or decays by half. A common definition for *half-life* is "the time required for exactly half of the entity to decay."

Today, we are at the halfway point of our study, and just as entities as diverse as a puddle of water on our driveway and carbon-14 have a predicted half-life (carbon-14's is over five thousand years; I hope that puddle won't last that long), so we must realize that our faith and determination to shine for God are subject to decay. Perhaps a few of us have even considered giving up on this idea of learning to be the light of the world, but today we will reaffirm our commitment by saying there is no place in our lives for "half-life Christianity." We will instead fight our tendency to slip, fall away, slide back into complacency, and all the other words and phrases that describe our natural tendency to drift from our spiritual moorings.

— • —

We all recall the feeling when we drove for the first time alone. What a thrilling adventure! Or how about the ecstasy of buying a new car? After six months, though, the car loses its new-car smell and we no longer park at the end of the lot to avoid door dings. In time that thrilling new car becomes just the vehicle that gets us from point A to point B.

Or how about the first date? A first kiss brought with it the thrill of new love, but the passion fades and a relationship is difficult to sustain.

"Familiarity breeds contempt" is a very old phrase and reflects the fact that if we are not intentional about cultivating friendships and intimate relationships, they decay just as surely as a radioactive element.

So it is with our faith. We remember how we felt when we truly heard the gospel for the first time. We recollect the thrill of discovery as we read through Scripture for the first time and its truth penetrated the very fiber of our being. Our prayers were fervent, our desire for God unwavering. But we can grow numb to anything, even God's Word. We can get to the point that we sit in church and go through the motions, but nothing touches us. We have allowed life to steal away our first love, and we need to commit to time with the Lord every day to regain what is lost.

It seems as though many pastors today are at risk of a half-life ministry. A recent *New York Times* article indicated that "members of the clergy now suffer from obesity, hypertension and depression at rates higher than most Americans. In the last decade, their use of antidepressants has risen, while their life expectancy has fallen."[2] While statistics about "pastor burnout" are not always reliable, existing studies show that burnout rates hover at around 40 percent, with some 1,500 pastors leaving their ministries each month due to burnout, conflict, or moral failure. And as many as 57 percent of active pastors say they would leave the ministry if they felt they had somewhere else to go vocationally.[3]

Our nation is trending toward nonbelief, as was reported by the Barna Group recently in their "2015 State of Atheism in America." The data shows that it is "increasingly common among Millennials to dismiss religion, God, churches, authority, and tradition."[4] The recent book *Sticky Faith* reported that 40 to 50 percent of high-school seniors "fail to stick with their faith" after graduation.[5] In fact, despite strong growth in Latin America and Africa, Christianity is stuck in something of a rut, if you look at Christians as a percentage of world population. Christians were 34.5 percent of the global population in 1900, 33.3 percent in 1970, 32.4 percent in 2000, and 33.4 percent in 2015, with projections of 33.7 percent in 2025 and 36 percent in 2050.[6]

The Bible makes it clear that we are subject to losing our faith unless we are intentional in sustaining it. In the book of Galatians, the apostle Paul told the church that they were returning to their godless ways: "But now that you have come to know God, or rather to be known by God, how is it that you turn back again to the weak and worthless elemental things, to which you desire to be enslaved all over again?" (4:9, NASB).

The Galatians may have once been "radioactive" believers, but their spiritual decay was evident in their turning back to the things that once held them captive.

Perhaps the clearest biblical teaching about our tendency to falter in our faith comes from the parable of the sower, found in Mark 4. This parable, also called the parable of the soils, recounts four scenarios of someone scattering seeds; three of them end in failure—seemingly reflective of the "half-life" challenges of faith. In the first failure, the seed falls on the path and birds come and eat it. Jesus explained this group as people who hear the message but the Enemy steals what "was sown in their hearts" (verse 15, NKJV). As children of the light,

we have to let the understanding of God's Word captivate our hearts and penetrate our minds so that we do not give the Enemy a chance to steal away the
gift of faith that God has scattered into our hearts.

In the second scenario, some of the seed falls on rocky ground and grows
up quickly but then is scorched by the sun and withers. Jesus said this example
refers to people who "hear the word and at once receive it with joy. But since
they have no root, they last only a short time. When trouble or persecution
comes because of the word, they quickly fall away" (verses 16–17). This is "half-
life" Christianity personified! How many people—many dear to us—hear the
good news of love and redemption and initially receive it with gladness but then
fail to cultivate a sustainable faith and are soon just a statistic for the next book
on how Christianity is waning in our nation?

The last seed that fails to grow falls among the thorns, is choked by the
thorns, and dies (verse 7). Jesus explained the parable this way: the seed that
falls among the thorns refers to people who hear the word, "but the worries of
this life, the deceitfulness of wealth and the desires for other things come in and
choke the word, making it unfruitful" (verse 19).

Some of us are crippled by worry; others of us are enthralled by materialism. Most studies say that 85 percent of the things we worry about never happen, and money never fulfills us for long.[7] Yet we rarely realize that our passion
for God is dimming. We forget to pray for a day or two, our Bibles stay shut,
the sun rises and sets, and we have lapsed into half-life Christianity.

Radioisotopes with short half-lives are dangerous for the straightforward
reason that they can dose you very heavily (and fatally) in a short time. A Christianity that decays is dangerous because it threatens every area of our lives. Our
relationships, our work—everything is affected when we lose our passion for
the things of God.

The apostle Paul wrote to the Ephesian church that once burned brightly
as a light to others but was slipping into a muted half-life Christianity. His
words are just as true for us today:

At one time you lived in darkness. Now you are living in the light that
comes from the Lord. Live as children who have the light of the Lord in
them. This light gives us truth. It makes us right with God and makes
us good. Learn how to please the Lord. Have nothing to do with the
bad things done in darkness. Instead, show that these things are wrong.
It is a shame even to talk about these things done in secret. All things
can be seen when they are in the light. Everything that can be seen is in
the light. The Holy Writings say, "Wake up, you who are sleeping. Rise
from the dead and Christ will give you light." (Ephesians 5:8–14, NLV)

The light that Christ wants to give us is eternal. His light is not subject to
the decay that is an inherent part of our daily lives. Look at its power: It gives
"truth." It "makes us good." This is the light of the world that we must diligently seek.

— • —

We are halfway through our journey of shining more brightly than ever before,
and we will let each day be a living testament of worship to our God.

Learn to worship with your wounds, praise with your problems, move with
your mess, sing through the sorrow, and dance in the drought! A life guided
by intentional, ongoing sacrifice in worship will never be described as half-life
Christianity.

Because He Lives!

The Spirit of God, who raised Jesus from the dead, lives in you. And just as God raised Christ Jesus from the dead, he will give life to your mortal bodies by this same Spirit living within you.—Romans 8:11, NLT

When Jesus died, your past died.

    When Jesus died, your sins died.

    When Jesus died, your hell died.

    When Jesus died, your captivity died.

    When Jesus died, your failures died.

But when Jesus rose, when He got up . . .

    Your salvation came to life.

    Your deliverance came to life.

    Your healing came to life.

    Your light came to life.

    Your peace came to life.

So now go with His resurrection power and bring life to the broken, bring life to the hurting, bring life to the dead around you.

The Inefficiency of Incandescence

While God does not remember our sins,
He never forgets His promises.

When most of us think of light, the first image that pops into our heads is that of the iconic light bulb, which has become synonymous with everything from bright ideas to the glitz of New York's Broadway. The standard bulb, also called an incandescent light bulb or light globe, is generally associated with the brilliant Thomas Edison, though historians list as many as twenty-two inventors prior to Edison as creators of the incandescent bulb.

While Edison's bulb was clearly not referenced when Christ called His followers the "light of the world," it is not too fanciful to think that He who is not bound by time saw this future invention as He spoke to His contemporary audience and to us, many generations later.

The incandescent bulb has a number of elements that parallel and deepen our understanding of how light can be transformative. As we shine God's love, we should be aware of the light and heat we transmit to the world, striving to illuminate truth and grace everywhere.

As author Ernest Freeberg wrote, "For more than a century Americans have regarded the creation of the incandescent light as the greatest act of invention in the nation's history."[1] Thomas Edison's relentless pursuit of a permanent replacement for arc lamps, candles, and kerosene transformed our nights into day and has had an overwhelming cultural impact that continues more than one hundred years later. Edison and others knew they were close to a break-through but needed something to handle the heat of an electric current when placed in a vacuum and enclosed in a glass bulb. They were able to perfect a carbon filament that worked, but the light bulb then and now was very ineffi-cient, throwing off far more heat than light.

As early as 1894, one *New York Times* reporter exclaimed, "What a pre-posterous dissipation there must be of the energy stored in a lump of coal be-tween its first liberation by combustion and its final emergence in the form of electric light!"[2] The inefficiency of incandescence has been chronicled for years, as the standard Edison screw-in bulb has been derided for using only 10 percent of its energy for light and the rest for heat. Many experts estimate that 10 to 15 percent of our electric bills are attributable to these wasteful though popular bulbs. According to the Natural Resources Defense Council, if all of the four billion light-bulb sockets in the United States contained compact fluorescent or LED lights, thirty coal plants' worth of power could be saved.[3]

As I write this book, a new era in lighting has begun. Mr. Edison's bulbs, which made kerosene and candles obsolete, are now swiftly becoming the stuff of antique shops and the occasional local hardware store. Congress ordered them phased out in 2007, and manufacturers stopped making them as of December 31, 2013, so when the supply runs out depends on your store's inven-tory and the continuing allure of Thomas Edison's 1879 invention. While there are a number of new lighting choices for consumers, most experts say the future is with light-emitting diodes, or LEDs, which are extremely efficient, though initially costly.

A 40-watt-equivalent LED is roughly ten times the price of the modern version of Edison's bulb but is still a bargain for the consumer in the long run. They are 85 percent more efficient and will last a lot longer. Instead of the standard 1,000 hours for an Edison bulb, these new bulbs will last for years. The industry joke is to buy one when you have a baby and replace it when the same child comes home from college. LEDs are also cooler to the touch and emit a pleasant soft light.

The story of Mr. Edison's bulb is a living metaphor for people of faith. The popular brand of faith—the religious parallel to the Edison light bulb—can often initially transform a community, but God is looking for one that is sustainable and contains more light than heat. Churches across our nation are realizing that we need LED-inspired efficiency to truly reach our communities. The incandescence of flashy worship services, "relevant" but shallow youth-group meetings, and Bible studies that are little more than fellowship over a glass of wine must be phased out and replaced with "sticky faith practices" that require more sacrifice and substance.

It will take years to phase out the old bulbs contained in billions of light sockets, and it will take years for a generation of churches with "new wineskins" to replace models that did not reflect the effulgence of God's truth and light. Yet a new hunger for God's unfiltered Word and orthodox teaching is transforming church communities throughout the United States and beyond. Worship services are focusing more on joining together in deep communion through music and less on entertainment value. New biblically focused and rigorous Sunday schools are replacing older models and challenging students of all ages to see God's transforming truths afresh.

One of the reasons the incandescent bulb has remained so popular is that it is familiar and casts a lovely, even flattering, light that creates a warm glow while brightening our homes. But it is fulfilling only 10 percent of its purpose, to be light.

Similarly, it is easy to fall into a faith that becomes like our favorite sweater. It is comfortable. Perhaps too comfortable. God will shake us from our comfort to ensure that we as His children are fulfilling more than 10 percent of our calling. A comfortable faith can be an inefficient faith. A comfortable church almost never fulfills its high calling.

Mr. Edison's light bulb was transforming. Our faith in Christ is transforming as well. The light bulb forever changed our perceptions of day and night. Jesus came so that we would see God differently—and forever. Edison's light bulb was basically a hot filament inside a vacuum that produced far more heat than light. Our faith can easily follow suit, expressed in a Christian vacuum of ideas and opinions and producing more heat (in the form of ideological debate) than light (the power of the risen Savior).

When Edison died in 1931, President Herbert Hoover requested that at 7:00 p.m. Pacific time—the hour when the sun would have set over the entire country—the nation turn off all its lights simultaneously for one minute and plunge itself into darkness. Radio stations across the nation would announce the moment. "This demonstration of the dependence of the country upon electrical current for its life and health," the president declared, "is in itself a monument to Mr. Edison's genius."[4]

As profound as Thomas Edison's invention was, it still was just a tool for humanity and has now become obsolete in our new world of greater light efficiency. Towering above Edison's accomplishment is a God who spoke light and life into being. He has given us the gift of eternal life and a way to defeat darkness and live for Him. Edison's power to reason and discover emanated from Him, the source of all truth and the embodiment of goodness.

It's not about my will, dreams, or aspirations. It's about Jesus—His purpose, passion, and promise. It's His agenda, not mine.

The light God has given us can never be obsolete. There is no more efficient or powerful version to come in the future. It is the transcendent, eternal light that brings hope to the hopeless and lights the way for the lost. It is that beacon on the rocky shore that announces danger and the laser that intercepts weapons that are meant to harm us.

One of the definitions for *incandescent* is "aglow with ardor and purpose." That is the kind of incandescence we want associated with our lives! To be filled with passion and purpose, not the inefficiency that defines many lives of faith. Our great God has given us His very Word as a lamp that guides our path and can never be extinguished.

As our journey continues, may we glow with His perfect message of beauty and grace, truth and compassion.

It's the Right Time!

The people of Beth-shemesh were harvesting wheat in
the valley, and when they saw the Ark, they were overjoyed!
—1 Samuel 6:13, NLT

God will bring you in when everything is ready! This is your harvest
season. This is your season to reap what you sowed for years! "So
let's not get tired of doing what is good. At just the right time we will
reap a harvest of blessing if we don't give up" (Galatians 6:9, NLT).

This is the word for you today: *it's the right time!*

It's the right time for your holiness.

It's the right time for your faith.

It's the right time for your family to be saved.

It's the right time for your deliverance.

It's the right time for your healing.

It's the right time to speak truth.

It's the right time to welcome the stranger.

It's the right time to shine the light!

17

"Light Bringers" for a New Generation

When you serve God with what you *have*,
He will give you what you *need*.

In February 1954, a navy pilot set out on a night-training mission from a carrier off the coast of Japan. While he was taking off in stormy weather, his directional finder malfunctioned, and he mistakenly headed in the wrong direction. To make matters worse, his instrument panel suddenly short-circuited, burning out all the lights in the cockpit.

The pilot "looked around . . . and could see absolutely nothing; the blackness outside the plane had suddenly come inside." Nearing despair, he looked down and thought he saw a faint blue-green glow trailing along in the ocean's ebony depths. His training had prepared him for this moment, and he knew in an instant what he was seeing: a cloud of phosphorescent algae glowing in the sea that had been stirred up by the engines of his ship. It was the "least reliable and most desperate method" of piloting a plane back onto a ship safely, but the pilot—future Apollo 13 astronaut Jim Lovell—knew that was precisely what he needed to do. And so he did.[1]

While he did not articulate it this way, Jim's life was saved because of light. Not just any light, but "bioluminescent dinoflagellates," which are tiny unicellular creatures that contain luciferin, a generic term for the light-emitting compound found in organisms that generate bioluminescence.

In his book that recounts this terrifying episode, Jim Lovell did speak of God and His influence, but more often he called himself lucky to have survived. I would say that Providence was at work, using a most unexpected light to guide him to safety.

— • —

How many people surround us daily who are in a spiritual condition that mirrors Lovell's dilemma? They are in a spiritual storm but "take off" each day into a world where the darkness they perceive closes in on their entire existence. The gloom creeps into their most intimate spaces, the "cockpits" of their lives, and they are desperate to find a way to "pilot their planes" to some safe harbor of hope. What will light their journey when they look into the blackness all around them? When their eyes adjust to the darkness, what life-saving light will they see?

Bioluminescent organisms live throughout the ocean, from the surface to the seafloor, from near the coast to the open ocean. In the deep sea, bioluminescence is extremely common, and because the deep sea is so vast, scientists say that bioluminescence may be "the most common form of communication on the planet."[2]

We primarily see bioluminescence triggered by a physical disturbance, such as the ocean's waves or a moving boat hull that gets the animals to show off their light. These tiny creatures also often light up in response to an attack or in order to attract a mate.

Many of us have seen the shimmer of fireflies on a summer's night. Fireflies are—like the dinoflagellate plankton that saved Jim Lovell—bioluminescent and produce light through a chemical reaction in their glowing abdomens.

Tracing the use of light by creatures in the sea is intriguing because as you descend, the sunlight disappears. First red light is absorbed. Then the yellow and green parts of the spectrum disappear, leaving just the blue. By a depth of seven hundred feet the ocean is in a continuous twilight. By two thousand feet, the blue fades out too. This means that most of the ocean is pitch dark. All day, all night.

— • —

To make light, you need three ingredients: oxygen, a luciferin, and a luciferase. A luciferin is any molecule that reacts with oxygen and in doing so emits energy in the form of a photon—a flash of light. A luciferase is a molecule that triggers the reaction between oxygen and the luciferin. In other words, the luciferin is the molecule that lights up, while the luciferase is what makes it happen. (Interestingly, Lucifer is a name for Satan that he had before his fall from heaven; in Latin it means "bringer of light.")

All these factors together make light uniquely useful as a weapon—or a veil. It can lure prey to you, or it can help you blend in. Producing a flash of light might also frighten a predator and create a chance to escape.

Satan, who is often called the Enemy, was once a "bringer of light." But instead of bringing light to God's throne in proper worship to the only King, he turned the spotlight on himself and in his radiance drew one-third of the angels with him. Light certainly can be mesmerizing and magical. But when the true Light shone in heaven, there was no room for an impostor. Satan was the bringer of light because he himself was not bioluminescent. His light was external, and the light of God was never fully in him. In the book of Isaiah God said, "I am the LORD, and there is none else. I form the light, and create darkness: I make peace, and create evil: I the LORD do all these things" (Isaiah 45:6–7, KJV).

Satan brought an empty, borrowed light that shone the way to destruction for all his followers, from angels to humankind.

We are called to be "light bringers" to a new generation. Just as creatures in the ocean respond to the depths in which they live, we must respond to our individual communities to bring a light tailored to their unique needs. That is the power of the light of Christ. It can bring hope and truth both to the surface dwellers and to those living in the blackest depths of the ocean floor. His light finds us where we are, in shade and light, in darkness and in twilight, and brings the only light that is life. His light must be our light.

The Bible says that "Satan disguises himself as an angel of light" (2 Corinthians 11:14, NLT). The deceptive light of the Enemy makes it all the more critical for us to be the bioluminescent light that guides people to God. Who today is sinking into a new depth, moving from yellow to green, then blue to black? Who is starting their day in a storm of physical abuse, as the darkness of anger and pain blackens every aspect of life? Have they been in darkness so long that their eyes have adjusted and they fail to see the light around them?

We are that light, the light of the world! If bioluminescent creatures need oxygen, a luciferin, and a luciferase to shine, we need these three ingredients: the Spirit of God, a willing heart, and the determination to bring His light to the oceans of darkness around us.

— • —

You may remember the name Jose Henriquez, a man who "helped his companions go from darkness into the light." *CBN News* shared the story of his dramatic rescue from a Chilean mine in 2010. The media gave him the title of "The Pastor," or "Spiritual Guide," but Henriquez prefers to be called simply Don Jose.[3]

At the time of the disaster—when the miners were trapped two thousand feet underground—Don Jose had worked in the mines for thirty-three years, the same amount of time he'd been married to his wife, Hetiz. There were also thirty-three miners trapped in the San Jose mine. The demanding ordeal received extensive media coverage, but a less reported fact was that Don Jose led devotions with the miners twice daily when they all cried out to God for a rescue. When rescue came, Don Jose was the first to go back into the mine to "return to thank God for getting him out of the depths of the earth alive." After a hero's reception in his hometown of Talca, Don Jose said, "The true hero is

Jesus Christ. . . . Apart from whatever man may have done both inside and outside that mine, He is the one who deserves the honor and the glory."[4]

Jose Henriquez was a bioluminescent force in that mine because he brought the peace and hope of Christ in the midst of an unthinkable situation. He did not allow the literal darkness or the bleakness of his circumstances to define his response. Instead, Henriquez focused on the light of Christ that cannot be contained, and he was the light bringer to his fellow miners.

The light of his story still illuminates today and inspires us to Be Light, to never give in to the darkness, to seek out those around us in need of hope, and to be a light bringer to this generation.

--- Reflection ---

What Do Christians Do?

The light shines in the darkness, and the darkness can never extinguish it.—John 1:5, NLT

When asked, "What do Christians do besides going to church on Sunday?" I answered:

We love.

We forgive.

We turn the other cheek.

We bless our enemies.

We walk in integrity.

We quench the thirsty.

We clothe the naked.

We feed the hungry.

We welcome the stranger.

We take care of the orphan and the widow.

We preach in and out of season.

We worship in spirit and truth.

We do justice.

We love mercy.

We walk humbly before God.

We are light.

When righteousness meets justice, Christ is exalted, truth stands revealed, hope arises, faith moves mountains, and His followers change the world. God changes us so we can change the world!

The Lightning Flash

What you survived last season
will determine what you will
conquer this season.

N o discussion of light is complete without a discussion of its most destructive form: lightning. Lightning strikes, lasting less than a half-millionth of a second, are explosions that shake the earth and bring destruction. The average lightning bolt can instantly boil 250 gallons of water and is hotter than the sun's surface. Summer skies in the United States generate 50,000 lightning flashes per hour, and 240 thousand people worldwide are injured by lightning every year.[1]

Lightning has often been associated with the supernatural. Lightning flashes from God's throne in the book of Revelation, and lightning preceded the giving of the Ten Commandments to Moses. The witches in *Macbeth* promise to meet "in thunder, lightning, or in rain."[2] Zeus's weapon was a lightning bolt. The Aztecs saw lightning as one of the many powers of their god. Captain Marvel and The Flash are among the superheroes who sport a lightning bolt as a symbol of their powers.

Roy Cleveland, a ranger at Shenandoah National Park in Virginia, survived a record seven lightning strikes between 1942 and 1977. As amazing as that might sound, statistics indicate that 90 percent of lightning-strike victims survive. Over the past three decades, lightning has killed an average of fifty-one people per year in the United States, but more than five hundred have survived.[3]

According to an article in *Outside* magazine,

> [Some] survivors awaken into temporary blindness or deafness, some-
> times the concussive force of the strike—or the electricity itself—
> ruptures eardrums. Some victims report the taste of metal on their
> tongues. Now and then, survivors develop strangely beautiful pink
> and brown bruises known as Lichtenburg figures, which look like
> intricate henna tattoos of branching fronds. These bruises likely
> trace the path of electricity that forced blood cells out of capillaries
> into more superficial layers of skin.[4]

— • —

We are called to be the light of the world, and so we must know light in all its forms. Because faith involves spiritual components of our lives, it can some-times be explosive and even destructive. In our zealousness to share the truth and power of God's love, we can sometimes overwhelm others with a sudden explosion of ideas that are foreign to them. Many people have become victims of a "lightning strike faith," which has scarred them as fully as one who sur-vived a lightning strike.

Many claim they have been burned by a religion that preaches hellfire and damnation instead of love and peace. Others say their faith was scorched by the materialism and hypocrisy they found in the church. Still others express they were victims of a church community that tried to dictate their behavior instead of accepting them for who they were.

My initial reaction to those kinds of complaints is that they often are words that conceal more than they reveal. People who react this way to faith are often trying to protect themselves from the shock and destruction of self that must take place to serve God fully.

In many ways, God comes to us like a lightning strike: He is sudden. He is out to destroy anything that keeps us separate from Him. He will drive out darkness in a flash of light and heat that rumbles the ground beneath us, shocks us into a new view of reality, and puts His mark of indelible love upon us. God demands no less than everything. Frankly, it is easier to criticize the perceived flaws in churches or individuals than give ourselves fully to a faith that is destined to course through every cell like the "10,000 wasp bites from the inside out," which lightning-strike victims describe when they are hit.[5]

The faith that empowers you to move mountains is the same faith that enables you to stand still. Therefore, stop trying to understand God and why difficult things happen, and start trusting God and watch great things happen.

"I will say of the LORD, 'He is my refuge and my fortress, my God, in whom I trust'" (Psalm 91:2).

— • —

Beyond its powerful beauty, lightning presents science and people of faith with one of its greatest mysteries: How does it really work? It is common knowledge that lightning is generated in electrically charged storm systems, but the exact method of cloud charging still remains elusive. The "storms of life" are a present reality as sure as tomorrow's sunrise. I recently spoke to a colleague and friend whose life has been fractured. She wept and spoke of her marital struggles—a husband who had promised to return from a trip out of the country in one month but was still gone three months later. Her students had been cruel that week, and colleagues had bruised her to the point that she was questioning her calling as a teacher. Her vulnerability crashed through the phone: "His peace is mine, but His joy remains elusive. I am His daughter, but I feel alone."

Thankfully, God held my tongue, which was filled with empty platitudes, and we prayed together as two pilgrims destined for the same port but separated by pain and our places in the journey.

Though rare, lightning can strike more than three miles from a storm, a "bolt out of the blue." Likewise, there are times spiritually when a brilliant flash of God's presence is needed to foster a lasting impact. The apostle Paul was completely blind to the truth of God's love. He watched in passive acceptance as Christians were massacred for their faith. He was so full of hatred that he was "breathing out murderous threats" against these new Christians, known as people of the Way (Acts 9:1). He was on his way to the city of Damascus, armed with letters from the high priest so that he could arrest any believers he encountered. Then lightning struck:

> As he neared Damascus on his journey, suddenly a light from heaven flashed around him. He fell to the ground and heard a voice say to him, "Saul, Saul, why do you persecute me?" . . .
> Saul got up from the ground, but when he opened his eyes he could see nothing. So they led him by the hand into Damascus. (verses 3–4, 8)

Paul was blinded by the light but could finally see the truth of God's presence. He would never be the same and emerged from his lightning experience as a man inflamed with God's love for others—transformed from a Christ hater into the epitome of a Christ follower.

— • —

There are many myths about lightning (such as it never strikes the same place twice—it actually strikes the same place repeatedly; just ask the night watchmen at the Empire State Building), but one truism is that current always chooses the path of least resistance.

I want to be that path when God is the current! When we resist evil and are open to God, we make ourselves lightning rods for His power! A lightning rod does not attract lightning (another myth). Instead, it has the ability to handle the enormous electrical current associated with the strike. Lightning rods are conduits for the power of the strike to safely find its way to the ground. Science says that if the lightning strike comes into contact with a material that is not a good conductor, the material will suffer massive heat damage.

So, are we good conductors of God's powerful love, transmitting it safely to others who will be forever transformed by His power?

We have already made it clear that God can use lightning-like events in our lives to shake us to our core and that He can use us as human lightning rods to safely convert a message that could be destructive into one that is life giving. The National Weather Service advises that there is no safe place outside in a thunderstorm, but the Lord is a haven in any storm:

> God is our refuge and strength,
> A very present help in trouble.
> Therefore we will not fear, though the earth should change
> And though the mountains slip into the heart of the sea;
> Though its waters roar and foam,
> Though the mountains quake at its swelling pride. (Psalm 46:1–3, NASB)

One of the most common pieces of advice regarding lightning safety is "Never lie down on the ground." After lightning strikes the ground, there is an electric potential that radiates outward from the point of contact in a way that might be deadly. Yet our God makes us "lie down in green pastures" and makes sure that we "shall not be in want" (Psalm 23:1–2). If it is His current that is coming, I seek to lie down and allow His Spirit to conduct a new power through my body—all for His glory.

Experts say that just before a lightning strike, our hair will stand on end, almost in anticipation of a violent flash. Lightning's power is unmatched in our world of light. No longer will we crouch in darkness, but we will wait in expectation for His current of love to come and transform us for His glory.

Blessed to Be Light by Where You Stand

Instead they put it on its stand, and it gives light to everyone in the house.—Matthew 5:15

The stand represents the facilitative platform from which we shine the light of Christ.

The question must be asked, "Where do we stand?"

We stand on the undeniable and unshakable truth that Christ is the Hope of Glory.

We stand with uncompromised and unbridled conviction; this may not be politically correct, but we stand on John 10.

We stand by proclaiming, "There are not five ways to heaven, four ways, three ways, or two ways. There is only one way to heaven, one way to eternal life, one way to salvation. And that way is Jesus Christ!"

We stand on righteousness and justice. The same God who pointed to righteousness via tablets of stone likewise imparted redemptive justice through Jesus's sacrifice on the cross. He wrote the law with one finger and grace with both hands.

To Be Light, we must stand with the understanding that Uncle Sam may be our uncle, but he will never be our heavenly Father!

Celestial Light

You can't speak like heaven
and look like hell, and you can't
speak like hell and look like heaven.

Emanuel Swedenborg was a noted scientist and inventor when on Easter weekend of 1744 he began having strange visions and dreams. These visions marked a turning point for Swedenborg, who would never return to science but instead became a mystic and religious figure with a small but devoted following.

Among the many religious topics he covered was a commentary on the rainbow in Genesis, which he related to what he termed "celestial light":

> These colors are from the light of heaven, and from the variegation
> of spiritual light. For angels live in light so great that the light of the
> world is nothing in comparison. The light of heaven in which angels
> live, in comparison with the light of the world, is as the noonday light
> of the sun in comparison with candlelight. . . . In heaven there are both
> celestial light and spiritual light. Celestial light—to speak compara-
> tively—is like the light of the sun, and spiritual light is like the light of
> the moon, but with every difference according to the state of the angel
> who receives the light.[1]

Swedenborg, like many others, was fascinated with the light of the heavens, often called celestial light. Poet William Wordsworth was drawn in as well and wrote:

There was a time when meadow, grove, and stream,
The earth, and every common sight,
    To me did seem
Apparell'd in celestial light.[2]

One book claims that celestial light allowed Adam to "survey the world from end to end." The text also claims that "the celestial light was but one of the seven precious gifts enjoyed by Adam before the fall and to be granted to man again only in the Messianic time."[3]

Meteors are celestial lights that were also misinterpreted for centuries. Shakespeare, like his contemporaries, saw them as "prodigies, and signs, abortives, presages, and tongues of heaven."[4]

In ancient times, rocks that supposedly had fallen from the sky were displayed prominently in many Greek and Roman temples. Such a black stone of meteor origin is displayed in Mecca in the Ka'ba, the holiest shrine of Islam. The legend is that Abraham the patriarch received the stone from the angel Gabriel. Later the stone passed in to the possession of Mohammed who placed it in the wall of the Ka'ba.[5] The power and beauty of light lead many to misidentify the source of light and begin confusing the light with other things, including the Light Giver, God.

The Bible has many references to a heavenly or celestial light. Among them is Paul's description in his first letter to Timothy, when he wrote about the "Lord of lords, who alone is immortal and who lives in unapproachable light, whom no one has seen or can see" (6:15–16). This "unapproachable light" is created by God as a reflection of His glory and an attribute of His nature.

In the *Evangelical Dictionary of Biblical Theology*, the authors clarified the distinction between the Creator and His creation, light:

Light is the first of the Creator's works, manifesting the divine operation in a world that is darkness and chaos without it. While light is not itself divine, it is often used metaphorically for life, salvation, the commandments, and the divine presence of God.[6]

— • —

As the light of the world, we must expose deceptive references to light and continue to point everyone to Jesus, who came as the Light of the world, destroying darkness through His sacrifice on the cross. We have learned—some of us the hard way—that Satan can disguise himself as an angel of light. We must live in the true light of salvation and, as Paul tells us, "put aside the deeds of darkness and put on the armor of light" (Romans 13:12). We know that "once you were darkness, but now in the Lord you are light. Live as children of light—for the fruit of the light is found in all that is good and right and true" (Ephesians 5:8–9, NRSVCE).

When God initiated His covenant with Abraham (then called Abram), He had him look up into the celestial light of the stars. God used the stars as symbols of His promise to bless Abram, the ancient childless patriarch, with many descendants. God also asked Abram to count the stars. Did this seventy-five-year-old man stand outside in night's darkness and lift his eyes heavenward and begin counting? What we know for certain is that as Abram looked at the stars, he believed God. This germ of eternal faith touches all generations, including our own, beckoning us to see the celestial light of these stars—we are those stars, descendants of Abraham by faith, crying out to him from the future as the enduring light we are to pass on to others.

We are the light of the world, and we must use the light of faith as armor to protect us from unbelief and as a weapon of spiritual warfare against the Enemy, who lives in, loves, and promotes darkness. If Abram had not looked up but instead continued to live as a wanderer and gave up on having a child because he and his wife were far beyond life-giving years, he would have missed the promise of the celestial light of faith. The moment he looked up to the sky, he became the model of a person of faith, a person who never allows circumstances to define his or her relationship to God but instead relies only on His Word, which strengthens his or her faith in the light of truth.

— • —

With all the light in our world, from the celestial light that shines from above to the light that shines out from our glittering cities, it is easy to be distracted from our clear call: Be Light to make luminous the world, to ignite everyone around us with the hope that comes from above.

In our busy world, it is rare for us to take a moment some evening, find a quiet spot away from the city lights, and gaze up into the heavens. We may feel the emptiness that can come with the vastness of the night sky. We might sense the wonder that the complexity of the galaxies brings. Perhaps by lifting our eyes into the celestial light above, we will feel our deep connection with the Creator, the One who made us in His image—which must include the light we share— and the One who said, "Let light shine out of darkness" (2 Corinthians 4:6).

When you walk with God in private, He shines on you in public.

Your days of darkness are over.

Shine, child of God, shine!

The Born Identity

You are all children of the light and children of the
day. We do not belong to the night or to the darkness.
—1 Thessalonians 5:5, NIV 2011

What are you?

You are what you pray.

You are what you see.

You are what you say.

You are what you think

You are what you hear.

You are what you do.

Then Jesus shows up and says:

"You are what I say."

"You are what I see."

"You are what I already did."

"You are what and who I say you are."

Which means what? It means you are

Anointed, appointed, and approved.

Bought, built, and blessed.

Called, forgiven, free, and favored.

A disciple, a worshiper, and a temple.

And above all . . . *you are His!*

The Brightest Magnetic Objects

Whatever you give to God,
He will crucify it, resurrect it,
deliver it, heal it, or multiply it.

O n December 27, 2004, astronomers detected a flash of energy from across our Milky Way galaxy so powerful that it bounced off the moon and lit up earth's upper atmosphere.

The flash, which lasted more than one-tenth of a second, was brighter than anything ever detected from beyond our solar system. NASA and European astronomy satellites and many radio telescopes on earth recorded the flash. Scientists later determined that the flash of energy came from a magnetar—the neutron star SGR 1806-20—some fifty thousand light-years away in an area of earth's sky known as the constellation Sagittarius.

Its apparent magnitude was brighter than a full moon and all previously recorded star explosions. Most of the energy was in invisible gamma rays, which are far more energetic than visible light or x-rays. For one-tenth of a second, the giant flare unleashed more energy than the sun emits in 150,000 years.

Like all these strange phenomena, magnetars are relatively tiny (about seven miles across), are extraordinarily dense (a teaspoon of neutron-star material would weigh about a billion tons on Earth), and have extremely powerful magnetic fields.

To those of us called to be the light of the world, magnetars represent something of an aspirational goal: In serving Christ, don't we want to be the brightest and most magnetic objects in the universe? Science tells us that magnetism is light and that magnets attract each other because they exchange the particles that make up light. But unlike the photons streaming out of a desk lamp or reflecting off everything you see around you, these photons are virtual and your eyes can't see them.

So, as the light of the world, we can attract others to God using invisible light (magnetic forces) and the visible light (kindness, grace, and mercy) that emanate from our Savior and shine through us. It can work like this: Jesus said, "I, when I am lifted up from the earth, will draw all men to myself" (John 12:32). Christ is the ultimate spiritual magnet. He was lifted up on the cross, where even death could not pull Him down. And we must continue to lift Him up by shining our light upon His sacrifice of love.

When you are full of what comes from heaven, you can confront the things that come from hell.

No one can resist the pure vision of the suffering Christ, shedding His blood for our sins so that we can finally be reconciled to God. His arms outstretched to the east and west, extended in the greatest act of compassion ever recorded.

The magnificent preacher Charles Spurgeon pointed out in one of his orations that Christ's death—intended to "end His influence among men"—had the opposite effect:

> Here is an amazing thing. The Lord Jesus has lost no influence by
> having been hanged upon the Cross! No, rather it is because of His
> shameful death that He is able to draw all men unto Himself! His Glory
> rises from His humiliation! His adorable conquest from His ignomini-
> ous death! When He "became obedient unto death, even the death of
> the Cross," shame cast no shame upon His cause, but gilded it with
> Glory! Christ's death of weakness threw no weakness into Christianity!

Say rather that it is the right arm of her power! By the sign of suffering unto death, the Church has conquered and will conquer still! By a love which is strong as death, she has always been victorious and must, forever, remain so. When she has not been ashamed to put the Cross in the forefront, she has never had to be ashamed, for God has been with her and Jesus has drawn all men to Himself.[1]

And just as He drew all to Himself through His death, He will return in a flash of magnetic light that will announce His promised return. When speaking of this event, Jesus said, "For the Son of Man in his day will be like the lightning, which flashes and lights up the sky from one end to the other" (Luke 17:24).

The Second Coming is announced by, of all things—and we are not surprised—*light*. But if the flash from the neutron star SGR 1806-20 was brighter than anything ever detected in our universe, the return of Christ will dwarf that event, as every eye will see Him as He lights up the skies from every vantage point in His creation.

— • —

Pope Francis recently asked crowds in St. Peter's Square if God's love was a magnet for us: "We can ask ourselves: Where is my treasure? What is the most important reality for me, the reality that attracts my heart like a magnet? Can I say that it is the love of God?"[2] So many things draw us away from our Lord, tempting us, pulling us into orbits of drugs, fame, or some other "magnetic" force. Instead, we need to put Jesus Christ at the center of our lives so that His magnetic field of love will draw us into an eternal orbit around Him.

Michael Faraday, a remarkable nineteenth-century scientist, was the first to make the connection between magnetism and light. Before his work, they were seen as separate areas of study, but he demonstrated that light is made of electric and magnetic fields. Perhaps even more remarkable, he believed that underlying the unity of magnets and light is a greater unity that we might call God, although Faraday and others described it as "the theory of everything." Here is how Faraday expressed it in 1846:

> I have long held an opinion, almost amounting to conviction, in common I believe with many others of natural knowledge, that the various forms under which the forces of matter are made manifest have one common origin; or, in other words, are so directly and mutually dependent, that they are convertible, as it were, one into another, and possess equivalents of power in their action. In modern times the proofs of their convertibility have been accumulated to a very considerable extent, and a commencement made of the determination of their equivalent forces.[3]

We people of light also believe with Farraday that all the "forces of matter . . . have one common origin" but that Jesus is that origin, as "without him nothing was made" (John 1:3). While science may one day discover the connection between the mighty flash of neutron stars and the common origin of all matter, we know that the Creator—who dwells in unmatched light—made all matter, light and magnets, men and women.

Magnetars may have magnetic fields that are up to twenty thousand times stronger than our sun's, but Jesus draws us to Himself with a force greater than any hatred or opposition and beckons us to be planets that encircle His beauty in a galaxy of faith. Darren Walter put it this way: "Much as the opposite poles of magnets are drawn to one another, the opposite characteristics of Jesus Christ and those of sinful men and women pull us to Him."[4]

— • —

We are now two-thirds of our way through this journey whose end is simply another beginning, a further refinement of our calling to be the light of the world. We know more about the nature and complexity of light than we could have imagined, and it reveals the infinite variety of our great God.

The brightest light has not yet shone into this world. It will come when Christ returns, but until that day, He is counting on us—poor vessels that lack His magnetic power—to shine brightly for all to see. We are the light of the world, and we aspire to the power of magnetars as we cling to the One who made them, and us, to shine for His glory.

================ Reflection ================

Using Your Power

See, I have already begun! Do you not see it?—Isaiah
43:19, NLT

The power to let go is as important as the power to hold on.

Today is a good day to . . .

Let go of the past and hold on to the promise.

Let go of the failure and hold on to faith.

Let go of the sin and hold on to salvation.

Let go of the guilt and hold on to the glory.

Let them go forevermore and hold on for the ride of your life!

21

Light and Our Crown

Your testimony is proof
that the devil is a liar.

The brain is the human organ most in need of enlightenment. The transformation of the mind is the true method in which humanity becomes holy, as God is holy (see Leviticus 19:2). Holiness is something God is, and it is what we are being called to be.

When light enters the mind, darkness is overtaken. The remedy for dark thoughts is not merely positive thinking; it is the introduction of God's holy light into the mind so that mental patterns are transformed. When light is introduced, it does not slowly shine; the effect is immediate. Light exposes and expels darkness, but the damage of darkness, its habits, its scars, and its evasiveness slowly give way to a new template. A new standard for thinking becomes a new standard for living. Christ becomes a new space occupier and mental pacesetter.

The head is not only the place where the transformation begins but is also where the transformation will one day be complete. In Philippians 1:6 Paul reminded us that He who has begun a good work is faithful to complete it, and one day God will give each saint a crown. Although we do not know exactly what that crown will look like, we may pick up some clues from Scripture as well as other historical narratives. A *corona* (Latin for *crown*) is an aura of plasma that surrounds the sun and other celestial bodies. The sun's corona extends millions of miles into space and is most easily observed during a total solar eclipse, but it is also observable with a special telescope called a coronagraph.

In essence, it is as if the sun has a crown or halo. Early Christian artists depicted scenes, such as the transfiguration of Christ, where a halo was used to accentuate glory and holiness. Other paintings showed people differentiated from one another by halos.

Actually, all saints who have accepted the gift of salvation are washed in the blood of Christ, are changed, and deserve a halo! Where once they were children of darkness and belonged to a dark world, now they have become children of light and belong to the One who is light. Sainthood does not begin in the new life but begins when Christ makes life new.

God will give us this crown one day—might it be a crown (corona) of light? A halo, if you will? A literal manifestation of what has transpired within the person? The halo depicted in those early Christian art pieces represented the glory of God, and God's glory can rest only on those who are holy. Real holiness can occur only within the bonds of relationship with God. Light has also been used as a symbol of holiness, but only God is truly holy, and His holy light can be our crown once we have been purged of unrighteousness through His blood.

Paul referred to the crown to come in 1 Corinthians 9:24–27, which says,

Do you not know that in a race all the runners run, but only one gets the prize? Run in such a way as to get the prize. Everyone who competes in the games goes into strict training. They do it to get a crown that will not last; but we do it to get a crown that will last forever. Therefore I do not run like a man running aimlessly; I do not fight like a man beating the air. No, I beat my body and make it my slave so that after I have preached to others, I myself will not be disqualified for the prize.

Paul used the crown (halo) as a theme representing a type of reward believers will receive in the world to come. He described a race we are all engaged in.

In the city of Corinth, historians tell us of an Olympic-type event called the Isthmian Games. They were held the year before and the year after the great Olympic Games. Victors received a halo-type crown made first with celery and then later with pine.

Paul made an obvious observation with eternal overtones. He described the race in a manner in which his readers would put themselves among the runners. He stated that in a race every runner runs but that the reader (us) should be determined to run like a runner who wins. In order to do that we need to mimic the behavior of a winning runner not only on race day but on training day.

Does anyone see a winning runner's daily routine? Paul refers to the beating of one's body in order to not be disqualified. This is not a masochistic statement from a sadist; it is an image of one working out, working hard, and working on the only tool he or she will be using in the race: his or her body. This taming and training of the body is not an exercise in religious routine. It is the work done by a person who understands what it takes to achieve the goal.

So let's think of holiness and the pursuit of a crown in light of this passage. The runner does not work hard in order to gain a relationship with Christ and ultimately earn a crown. The runner works hard to develop the character of a champion. The glory of the crown becomes synonymous with the glory of the One who awards the crown. Jesus is the goal, and He awaits us at the finish line. The phases of the race become steps in becoming more like Him.

Paul stated that the crown sought after in these games is a corruptible crown. It will one day wither and probably be discarded. However, the crown that is placed on the winner of the race he referred to is a crown of glory given by the King of glory and will never see corruption. Simply stated, glory cannot be corrupted. When we understand that glory can come only from the God of glory, we then understand the eternal reward it represents.

Because glory cannot be corrupted, every person who has received God's glory will one day receive a glorified body. The individual receives both an incorruptible crown and an incorruptible body. What a glorious concept. While we wait for a crown of glory, God wants to initiate and introduce glory into the head that will one day wear a splendid crown.

This halo, this corona, this visual manifestation of a mind being transformed, being completed internally, is now depicted externally. The crown, the glory placed on the person, is now placed on the head to represent a person who has been glorified because of the ongoing work God has done on the inside.

The race and the process of transformation can be seen as synonymous. It is in the race, or in the journey, that a person is being perfected into the image of the One who awaits beyond the yellow tape. Holiness, then, is something that Christ has worked out and that we participate with in working out.

While the runners run, while they discipline their bodies, they go through this process of being refined. Likewise, holiness costs something. It cost Christ His life to provide the avenue of holiness, but it also is something that should cost the runner. So we "count the cost," we make the effort, we allow the transformative light to renew our mind, our body, and our spirit.

This is what Paul stressed in verse 25: everyone who competes in the games goes into *strict training*. They do it to get a crown that will not last, but we do it to get a crown that will last forever. This strict training is not popular in today's atmosphere of shortcuts and quick fixes. You cannot get in shape if someone else works out. You cannot be trained by default. *Everyone* means "everyone." Everyone must train, everyone must run, and everyone is responsible for his or her own race.

To Be Light and overcome darkness, we must allow the light of Christ to overcome our sinful nature. The mind can be either a dark room with hidden chambers of hidden secrets and false identities or a transformed vessel housing the light deposited by God. Darkness cannot be overcome on one's own, but when we accept His light, darkness surrenders. This light is at work in our minds but will one day be represented by a crown of light on our heads. Our faith stands measured not by our response when heaven falls upon us but rather by how we react when hell stands next to us.

You cannot Be Light unless you have light in you. You cannot give what you do not yet have. When talking about God's light, you cannot give what you are not. We must Be Light if we are ever going to expose others to light.

One day we will receive a corona, a crown of light. But if it is the first light we ever have, it will be too late for it to be of help to others.

Could it be that God wants us to have a crown of light that in reality is now and not yet? Should we not be keepers and wearers of light today and not only in the world to come? Can we run like a winner before crossing the finish line? We can, we must, we will. So wear your corona and wear it well.

God Knows Your Name

Fear not, for I have redeemed you;

　　I have called you by name, you are mine.

When you pass through the waters, I will be with you;

　　and through the rivers, they shall not overwhelm you;

when you walk through fire you shall not be burned,

　　and the flame shall not consume you.

For I am the LORD your God,

　　the Holy One of Israel, your Savior.—Isaiah 43:1–3, ESV

"Samuel!"

The same lips that uttered, "Let there be light!"

The same God who asked Adam, "Where are you?"

The same voice who announced Himself as "I AM" to Moses.

That same voice, the voice of the Creator, the omnipotent, omniscient, omnipresent Lord of the universe, invades the molecules of sound to penetrate the auditory walls of an unsuspecting young man resting in proximity of glory and utters one word: "Samuel!"

He could have introduced Himself and shouted, "It's Me, God!"

He could have been introduced by a host of angels.

Instead, His voice uttered one word: "Samuel!"

The profoundness of this expression cannot and should not be overlooked.

For God could have likewise called out, "Hey, you!" or "Mr. Sleepy!"

Get this: God didn't identify Samuel by his location (where he was) or by his youthfulness.

God connected with this man by simply saying, "I know you. I know you by name: Samuel."

God knows your name too.

God knows who you are.

God knows where you live.

God knows how you live.

God knows you—the good, bad, and ugly.

God knows your strengths and weaknesses, your fear and faith, your heaven and hell.

And He still loves you.

And He still has a plan for you.

And He still wants to bless you.

And He still wants to use you.

Why? Because He doesn't identify you by your past or by your circumstances.

He doesn't say, "Hey, you in the pit," or "Mr. Drug Addict," or "Mrs. Adultery," or "Madam Divorce," or "Mr. Unemployed."

No! When God calls you, His voice is intimate, affirming, and always graceful.

God knows you by name!

22

Let the Wind Blow on Us

The will to "hold on" and the power to "be still" are as important as the will to "let go" and the power to "move forward."

The aurora borealis, known more commonly as the northern lights, is a natural phenomenon that residents of the northern part of the earth enjoy. On special evenings the sky is lit up with an array of lights that no artist can duplicate on canvas.

The northern lights circle the northern part of our planet in an elliptical oval or circle. Think of light being blown in a circle around the top (northern) part of the earth.

It is believed that the north magnetic pole is slightly offset, so it unveils a phenomenon called the aurora oval. The magnetic pull creates an oval of light. The area of greatest auroral activity is directly under this oval.

Dynamic changes in the atmospheric light are directly affected by the course of solar wind. So depending on the flow of the wind, the northern lights may appear to be more brilliant and dynamic, and it may appear that the light is constantly moving in a circular motion or spinning.

Both scientific and legendary explanations for these lights, discovered by Galileo in 1619, illustrate how God uses light to make our world beautiful. The name itself expresses belief in a divine hand involved in painting an array of beautiful light. When we examine the distinct parts of the name, we launch into an interesting analysis. The word *aurora*, which in Roman mythology was the name given to the goddess of the dawn, reveals both human appreciation of and dependency on light. Dawn represents that a new day or new beginning has begun. For those who are seriously ill, it means they have lived through the night, the hours believed to be the most difficult to survive. For those who are well, it means one more opportunity to work, to be productive, and to worship God.

The writer of Lamentations expressed it poetically this way:

> The steadfast love of the LORD never ceases;
>   his mercies never come to an end;
> they are new every morning;
>   great is your faithfulness. (Lamentations 3:22–23, ESV)

The first light of day is that moment when the fullness of who you are as a human being—your body, your mind, and your soul—acknowledges God's mercy and His faithfulness. This light celebrates the joy and hope in facing a new day. As children of the light we are charged with the glorious responsibility of carrying this hope to brighten the world of those around us.

God's light not only overcomes the darkness in your life, but when carried and given to others it overcomes the darkness of the world. God calls His children to be like a new dawn for others by lighting up their world and demonstrating both hope and mercy. This is made possible through the inner working of the Holy Spirit and the outer overflow of the Spirit's presence in a believer's life.

Which leads me to the word *borealis,* the word in Latin for "wind." The image illustrated in the term *aurora borealis* is of wind blowing light against the backdrop of the night sky so that which is normally dark is lit up with dynamic color.

— • —

On day twenty-one we looked at the corona, or the crown, that saints will wear one day and in essence wear today. Now, as we look at the phenomenon of aurora borealis, it is almost as if God has provided a way to remind us that this world is His and the north or "head" of the planet demonstrates His glorious involvement in our world.

The creation story begins with the Spirit of the Lord hovering over the water. The Hebrew word for "Spirit" is *Ruach*, which roughly translated means both wind and spirit. The Hebrew word for "hover" is *MeRAChEFET*, which is used in Deuteronomy 32:11:

> Like an eagle that stirs up its nest
>> and hovers over its young,
> that spreads its wings to catch them
>> and carries them on its pinions.

God created the heavens and the earth, which lay until the utterance of that word, in the chaos of darkness and desolation. Was the scene something akin, possibly, to the all-pervasive electromagnetic activity of the aurora borealis that penetrates the chaotic night of the world? I propose that the aurora borealis can remind us of how God once hovered over the earth like an eagle that stirs up its nest. Yet God does not just stir up wind but stirs up light for His creation. Zechariah makes reference to the Spirit of God spinning in a way that reminds us of the light that seemingly spins on the aurora oval.

The prophet Zephaniah described a prophetic vision in which he saw a distinct way God interacted with His creation. He began with a bold declaration where he exclaimed, "The LORD your God is with you" (3:17). It would not be until the birth of Christ when Emmanuel—God with us—would become a reality. He would be heaven's ambassador, sent to announce that God has made His grand appearance to reconnect with His people. God sent the darling of creation to repair what seemed to be an irreparable chasm caused by those dearest to Him. He was now ready to rid the world of the depravity that comes with separation. He is the God that Zephaniah saw as being "with you," with us, and with all who would receive Him.

Zephaniah also exclaimed, "He will take great delight in you" (verse 17), a prophecy of a coming time when the jewel of God's creation would once more be in full relationship with the Creator. He proclaimed a coming day when people would have the ability, through Christ, to surrender themselves to God.

On that day God cannot help but delight in you and me. He delights in seeing His people restored. He delights in seeing His glory in His creation. We need to acknowledge that we serve a God who is delighted with, enamored with, in love with, excited about, and even ecstatic about His people!

He was so pleased that Zephaniah also revealed that "he will rejoice over you with singing" (verse 17).

This is the crème de la crème message, a statement that reveals God's passion for us that culminates in love that must be expressed in action.

The Hebrew word translated "rejoice" is *sus,* which can be translated to mean "to dance or to spin around with exuberance." The picture here is one of a Hebrew wedding where it was expected that people would not hold back their emotional joy. It is the type of occasion that brings so much passion that you just have to begin to spin and dance and possibly have a foolish expression of gladness!

This is not the kind of rehearsed dance one does in a performance nor a stylistic dance done for competition or ritual. This is a wild dance that spontaneously erupts when someone wins the prize, gets the girl, or is holding the winning ticket. When God thinks of you, and He does, He cannot help but break out in a spinning, dancing outburst!

This spinning is accompanied with a *rinnah* or "spontaneous song." God creates a beautiful melody that intentionally proclaims and expresses extreme joy. So the God of the universe, the Holy One, the King of kings and Lord of lords, sings and dances over you with a passion understood only by those who have lost their manners because of their love!

The ultimate expression of one who receives and possesses the light of God is the love of God. Before we rejoice in the Lord, He has already rejoiced over us. In essence we are involved in a spinning dance with God Himself. He rejoices in us as we rejoice in Him.

This is an exuberant dance, an "aurora borealis type" dance, if you will. When God spins, it causes the light of His glory to blow and create a beautiful array that lights up darkness. You have already overcome the darkness because the God who saves you loves you. He sings over you. He dances over you, and that dance brings light to whatever darkness has tried to defeat you.

Why are you still standing? Because God's plans for you are greater than all of hell's plans against you!

When the light of each new day comes (dawn, aurora) the wind (boreas) of the Holy Spirit should produce in us the spectacular effect of the northern lights. This means that God does not just dance over you, but when He overtakes your life He is dancing within you. You become a walking, talking northern light. Your mission is to bring joy to those around you because of the joy within you, to bring light to those around you because of the light within you, and to be both a recipient and a conduit of God's glory in this world.

Move!

The path of the righteous is like the first gleam of dawn,

shining ever brighter till the full light of day.

—Proverbs 4:18

Throughout Scripture, people experienced breakthroughs when they did something requiring faith. We don't sit by faith; we walk by faith. We don't recline by faith; we run by faith. *We move:*

Moses stretched

Joshua shouted

David threw

Elijah prayed

Esther touched

Zacchaeus climbed

And Peter stood up!

Get up and act on God's Word today. Why? Because you're not waiting for a miracle. There's a miracle waiting for you!

Earthquake Light

When God removes it, He always replaces it with something better.

The year was 1989 and the World Series, dubbed that fall as the "Battle of the Bay," was set to begin. The Giants were hosting their cross-bridge rival, the Athletics. The entire Bay and East Bay were abuzz with baseball. The Athletics led two games to zero after a brilliant pitching exhibition, and fans all over the world had their eyes glued to their television sets for game three.

At 5:00 p.m. announcers Al Michaels and Tim McCarver began their broadcast. The weather was perfect and though the A's were up in the series, the Giants were still expected to make a great showing. The beginning of the broadcast featured a brilliant video tribute to both baseball franchises. Everything about the evening was normal and routine.

At 5:04 p.m. the camera shot of the commentators was suddenly interrupted. The video disappeared from the screen, but the announcers could be heard saying, "I think we are having an earthquake." The network carrying the game did not know the gravity of the situation. *Just what was happening? Would the game continue?*

At first the fans at the game did not leave their seats. When the video signal came back, there was a scramble for the network to show both baseball and other breaking news. Soon it was evident that the earthquake was much more severe than the baseball commentators were aware.

Camera crews around the Bay Area made it possible for viewers to witness the strong effect of an earthquake in real time. For the first time in history on live television, people saw the raw power of what the shaking of the earth could produce. Although viewers could not feel the earthquake, they would soon understand the disruption to routine life caused by the Loma Prieta quake.

As the program segued to different scenes, viewers witnessed crumbled buildings and collapsed sections of bridges and freeways that had given way due to the swaying and rocking.

One of my close friends, Dr. Nick Garza, was living in the Santa Cruz Mountains at the time and described the fierceness of a 7.1 earthquake: "The feeling that there is nothing you can do to gain control, that there is nothing you can hold on to, and nowhere you can hide was astounding." The epicenter was approximately eight miles from his apartment, and though the actual earthquake was unsettling, so was the despair that came in the following days as normal routines were completely disrupted.

Earthquakes have a way of unsettling people who normally believe they have it all together. They are as disruptive and intrusive as they are destructive. Despair comes easily, sleep is troubled, and normality returns at a snail's pace.

In comparison to some of the earthquakes that have occurred overseas, the damage caused by the Loma Prieta quake seems almost insignificant. When earthquakes occur in third-world or underdeveloped nations, they cause massive turmoil. On January 12, 2010, a magnitude 7.0 earthquake struck Haiti. More than 160,000 people died and nearly 1.5 million others were displaced due to the overwhelming damage. The lack of infrastructure and differences in building materials and building codes resulted in the flattening of entire city blocks. Incredible organizations like Convoy of Hope responded quickly and today continue to bring hope to that devastated country.

On April 25, 2015, another devastating earthquake hit the mountainous nation of Nepal. News affiliates focused attention to a region of the world ill prepared for the destructive force. The quake caused an avalanche on Mount

Everest that killed at least nineteen people, including an executive from Google. Gripped by fear, many survivors slept in the streets, not wanting to be caught in an unstable building if aftershocks or another quake occurred. Like in San Francisco and Haiti, people dreaded the feeling of despair, as they had no control, especially within a building. Their only choice was to eat, sleep, and spend their time in what felt like the safety of the street.

The destructive power of these and other earthquakes throughout history has caused both horrific damage and incredible humanitarianism. As with many cataclysmic events, earthquakes seem to bring out the best in people. Human beings are made in the image of God, and like God humanity shines when darkness attempts to overwhelm.

— • —

There is an interesting phenomenon that is witnessed during an earthquake called "earthquake lights." People have observed this inexplicable light emitted during a quake, and research into what causes these lights is ongoing. Several mechanisms might explain the phenomenon. The most recent model suggests that the generation of earthquake lights involves the ionization of oxygen-to-oxygen anions by breaking peroxy bonds in some types of rocks due to the high stress before and during an earthquake. After the ionization, the ions travel up through the cracks in the rocks. These lights have been witnessed as either a flash or as an aura.

In more simple terms, all that shaking may actually cause electrical charges in rocks to be channeled to the surface through vertical faults in the earth. Friedemann Freund of San Jose State University and NASA's Ames Research Center explained that these lights can be seen as either blue flames that come out of and stay low to the ground or as floating balls of lightning that hover for seconds or even minutes. He also said that on some occasions these quick flashes of brightness appear as lightning strikes coming out of the ground and can stretch over six hundred feet.[1]

— • —

Psalm 19:1 states, "The heavens declare the glory of God; the skies proclaim the work of his hands." The psalmist was not making a random declaration about the beauty found in nature but was proclaiming that everything we see when we look at the sky announces or presents the glory of God. So it is interesting to consider that in the midst of something as chaotic as an earthquake, God may be reminding us that light is still present—that the glory of the Lord does not shrink back even when the earth is shaken.

Consider the application for your personal life: in the midst of the most chaotic shaking you have ever experienced, God's glory is evident. Consider also that during what you think is the most incredible personal earthquake, some of the most brilliant light in your life might be revealed! What you think has come to destroy you has come to produce light in you. Sometimes God will close the door—not to punish you—but to protect you from the elements that may hinder the fulfillment of your destiny.

What does God's glory in you look like?

To them God has chosen to make known among the Gentiles the glorious riches of this mystery, which is Christ in you, the hope of glory. (Colossians 1:27)

Glory is usually not produced when we go on vacation.

Glory is not only produced when life is solemn or peaceful, or when you have warm and happy thoughts.

God's glory is sometimes best revealed in the midst of what can seem the darkest of circumstances.

So how do we overcome darkness? We allow light to be produced in us. Light is produced through the pressure and the shifting of our own personal fault lines. The very cracks we may think we have can be the means God uses to expose His light.

Paul stated emphatically, "For since the creation of the world God's invisible qualities—his eternal power and divine nature—have been clearly seen, being understood from what has been made, so that men are without excuse" (Romans 1:20).

If God's invisible qualities and His eternal power are clearly seen in the rest of His creation, then shouldn't His invisible qualities, His glory, and His light be revealed in the part of creation that was made in His image?

One of the expressed purposes each of us has is to reveal His light, and His light is certainly released when the worse darkness envelops us: That earth-shaking illness exposes His hope and light. That divorce and heartbreak exposes His light. You might call your current shaking a 7.1 of life, but God is still God, light is still light, and light will surface in the midst of the shaking. Because what God has put in you will be exposed when the pressure is on!

In the midst of personal quakes, God has provided a peace "which surpasses all understanding" (Philippians 4:7, NKJV). It is a peace that someone holding the light of Christ has in reserve. In the midst of the storm, this is the peace that guards your heart and your mind. What is interesting about earthquake light is that it occurs just before or during the quake. Sometimes you need the light to show up during the turmoil, not just when things have stabilized.

In the midst of the infant church's early years Paul and Silas were imprisoned. Their crime was delivering a female slave from a spirit that gave her the ability to tell fortunes. Paul and Silas were locked in prison, where they sang songs to the Lord. Suddenly an earthquake shook the jail and all the cell doors swung open. Acts 16:29–30 says, "The jailer called for lights, rushed in and fell trembling before Paul and Silas. He then brought them out and asked, 'Sirs, what must I do to be saved?'"

Light brings hope. Earthquakes tell of the light to come. Things that shake your comfort level produce a light for your new beginning. The earth might be shaking, but the light is coming. The jail is shaking, but the light is coming. Your health might shake, but the light will come. Your relationships may shake, but call for a light. When Christ died the earth shook, and before He returns and His glorious light is revealed, Scripture prophesies that there will be many earthquakes. Ask yourself today: Do I trust God in the midst of my shaking? Do I believe His light will get me through this mighty shaking? Am I willing to allow others to see God's light in me in the midst of my chaotic situation?

Your Identity

Those who are wise will shine like the brightness of the heavens, and those who lead many to righteousness, like the stars for ever and ever.—Daniel 12:3

Saint, who are you?

Repeat after me:

I'm not what my critics say I am.

I'm not what my past says I am.

I'm not what hell says I am.

I'm not what my circumstance says I am.

I am what I AM says I am!

You will see what God says you will see!

You will reach what God says you will reach!

You will conquer what God says you will conquer!

You will reap what God says you will reap!

24

The Light of Massive Collisions

You must learn to "get over"
before you "take over."

M ay the force be with you."
This line from *Star Wars* in 1977 introduced a generation of new sci-fi enthusiasts to a concept of an unseen source of power or, more accurately, an unseen energy that was at work in an imaginary universe, out there somewhere, and yet was somehow part of every living being. The creative force behind *Star Wars*, George Lucas, wonderfully presented a story line that included a force with both a positive and a dark side—and he cashed in at the box office. As in many great stories, the forces Lucas introduced us to would collide in both a seen and an unseen world. This force seemed to tap into the imagination and human narrative of people all over the world.

It can be argued that fictional stories that mimic reality capture our attention more than those that borrow themes that do not. Some of the greatest stories depicted in film or in writing are often an attempt to explain the order of the universe or some other aspect of a faith narrative. *Star Wars* attempted to explain a source of power that many in humanity would recognize.

This chapter explores and relates spiritual principles to the concept of *annihilation*. Annihilation, also called pair annihilation, is the process in which a particle and an antiparticle unite, annihilate, and produce one or more photons. When an electron and positron annihilate, the total amount of energy available is about one billion electron volts! That's power!

The energy in a photon of visible light is about two to three electron volts. So if the electron and positron annihilate and make only two photons, the two photons each have hundreds of millions of times too much energy for your eye to even detect. And it is possible for the annihilation to produce many more than two photons!

Early in the first chapter of Genesis we are introduced to the first annihilation in history: "And God said, 'Let there be light,' and there was light. God saw that the light was good, and he separated the light from the darkness" (verses 3–4).

The annihilation that took place here was that initial moment that light collided with darkness. If we could travel back through time and see the brilliant effect of light at creation, it would be an incredible sight.

And as we've just discussed, the principle of annihilation states that more light is unseen than can be seen.

— • —

Humans tend always to correlate the natural with the supernatural.

Many ancient cultures worshiped natural occurrences or major natural objects, such as rain, thunder, sun, moon, stars, fire, water, mountains, and so on. You can argue that this is the basis of human fantasy, mythology, and all sorts of religious fabrications, or you can reason that there is something innate in the human experience that provokes people to give the credit for natural occurrences to supernatural causes or manifestations.

Even many of the staunchest atheists have admitted that there is what they deem "temptation" to believe that there must be a divine hand in creation— that the world's majestic beauty and complexity must have as its source a deity. Although they use this assertion as a set-up statement to then attempt to blow holes in divine creationism, they open the door to acknowledging an innate desire to tie together what can be seen with what cannot be seen. Again, humanity wants to discover connections between the natural and supernatural.

That incredible sight that would have been seen at the moment light was introduced in the creation is nothing in comparison to what would have occurred in the unseen. For every bit of light you would have witnessed chasing the earth's darkness, there would have been an immeasurable amount of light you could not see. What was this light doing? What was this light illuminating? What was the light making possible? What was this light colliding with?

At creation God was setting in order principles that would be imbedded throughout Scripture. Light introduced to a dark, void, and chaotic space generates potential for all kinds of things to occur. Where there is light things can live, grow, thrive, and bring transformation. The light also has the potential to collide with organisms that can absorb and release energy.

So what happens when the light of God collides with the darkness of the Enemy? The concept of annihilation gives us clues. When our Enemy (being like the electron) and we (being like the positron) annihilate, a tremendous amount of energy is released—most of which is not visible but is made up of the same stuff (photons) as visible light. Just as the unseen light would have been immeasurable at creation, we would not be able to quantify the amount of light or energy released in the conflict described in the book of Ephesians: "For we do not wrestle against flesh and blood, but against principalities, against powers, against the rulers of the darkness of this age, against spiritual hosts of wickedness in the heavenly places" (6:12, NKJV).

I have heard about, preached about, learned about, and been scared about the implications of this verse. An important question is how do we go about wrestling things we cannot see? How does one engage in a wrestling match with an invisible opponent? How do you go through experiences on earth that have implications beyond earth?

Just like the Hebrew boys in Daniel 3, it doesn't matter if you don't see God in the midst of what you're going through. What matters is that hell sees God in the midst of what you're going through.

I believe that understanding annihilation helps us understand this wrestling in heavenly places. We are God's children of light. We have been transformed to "open their eyes and turn them from darkness to light, and from the power of Satan to God, so that they may receive forgiveness of sins and a place among those who are sanctified by faith" (Acts 26:18). The evidence of being turned to light can be seen in this world, but it also has unseen effects.

Not only do we leave darkness but we are also engaged in a war with darkness—a war that feels very much one dimensional but that according to Scripture is actually multidimensional. In other words, the war or the struggle we are engaged in here is mirrored in heavenly places. The light produced by spiritual collisions that involve us also produces light and has spiritual consequences in heavenly realms. I propose that every time we are under spiritual attack, what we see manifested on earth dwarfs in comparison to what is manifesting in the heavens.

As we take on the forces of Satan, we must remember what the Word says about our foe, that he "masquerades as an angel of light" (2 Corinthians 11:14). He masquerades or mimics light, but he can neither produce nor reflect true light because he embodies darkness. We, on the other hand, are true carriers of God's light and have a real role in what occurs in heavenly realms. In fact, when we are attacked on earth, heavenly attacks are taking place. And when we are blessed on earth, heavenly blessings are taking place: "Praise be to the God and Father of our Lord Jesus Christ, who has blessed us in the heavenly realms with every spiritual blessing in Christ" (Ephesians 1:3).

This was also demonstrated when Simon declared Jesus was the Messiah: "Jesus replied, 'Blessed are you, Simon son of Jonah, for this was not revealed to you by man, but by my Father in heaven'" (Matthew 16:17). Here again we see a clear connection between Simon being enlightened by a heavenly connection although he is simply flesh and blood.

The battle is real. The earthly turmoil can be felt. However, something just as real is occurring in the heavenly dimensions "far above all rule and authority, power and dominion, and every title that can be given, not only in the present age but also in the one to come" (Ephesians 1:21).

We are truly citizens of heaven and His kingdom although we exist in this earthly dimension. "For he has rescued us from the dominion of darkness and brought us into the kingdom of the Son he loves" (Colossians 1:13).

The church also is multidimensional. Jesus promised that the gates of hell would not prevail against her (see Matthew 16:18). When the apostle Paul wrote his letter to the Ephesians, his intent was to make clear that through the church the manifold wisdom of God should be made known to the rulers and authorities in the heavenly realms (see Ephesians 3:10). This is a complicated Scripture passage. God associates with the church not only to do His will on earth but to take its position and role in heavenly realms! So this "city on a hill," this light that is meant to shine, is shining not only to effectively transform the world but to effectively bring light to battle darkness in unseen places.

This is an awe-inspiring but sobering reality!

— • —

The beginning of the movie *Gladiator* has always fascinated me. Maximus Decimus Meridius, who would later become an enslaved but famous gladiator, is commanding a Roman army in a battle with some Germanic tribes. During a speech he gives to his troops he shouts, "What we do in life echoes in eternity."

For the rest of the movie the gladiator, although enslaved, engages in a journey that will change the course of history. It is as if Maximus realized all along that what he did mattered. His life, battles, and actions had a visible effect in the natural world but also had future consequences far greater than what could be seen. He instilled this vision in his troops as well. He wanted every infantryman, horseman, archer, and water boy to understand that they were connected to a kingdom and a story line that was impacting something bigger, something not yet visible.

What we do here echoes in eternity! As agents of light we affect the seen and unseen realms. The warfare we are engaged in here is echoing in high places. The battle you are going through, that collision in your private world, creates a dynamic light that brings hope in your situation but also is mirrored and echoed in heavenly places. The Enemy ignorantly places God's children in places where they can conquer him in their private world and also annihilate him in the unseen world. You cannot have an obliterating annihilation without the colliding annihilation.

Although it would be unwise to welcome trouble, when it happens, know that the light of the world will be present in your situation and exalted in unseen places. Your deliverance brings an environment of deliverance around you. Your battle affects others who are in battles all around you.

As an agent of light, God has called you to realize that everything you go through produces light that flows through you. Darkness will not defeat you. You do not have to set out to defeat darkness, because darkness will be defeated when it collides with the light in you. You will have victory both in the seen and the unseen!

Anointed

Even the darkness will not be dark to you;

the night will shine like the day,

for darkness is as light to you.—Psalm 139:12

Without God's anointing, we can't confront principalities and powers of darkness. But with the oil, with the anointing, comes the miraculous:

With the anointing, Joshua knocked down the walls of Jericho.

With the anointing, Gideon defeated the Midianites.

With the anointing, David brought down the Philistine Goliath.

With the anointing, Solomon built the temple.

With the anointing, Daniel prophesied in the presence of an enemy king.

As the anointed, Jesus changed water into wine, walked on water, gave sight to the blind, resurrected Lazarus, cast out demons, went to the cross, then was resurrected and defeated the power of death, ascended, and sent us the Holy Spirit.

We can't shine our light,

knock down our walls,

defeat our overwhelming enemies,

bring down our giants,

build our temples, or

prophesy into power unless we have one thing:

God's anointing!

25

Lightships

*You have to learn to sing in the desert
before you dance in the promised land.*

Recently I have discovered part of the nautical world I was formerly not aware of. We have all heard of lighthouses, but many have never heard of lightships. To better understand the purpose and principles of lightships we need to first review the role of lighthouses.

Lighthouses are a historical and architectural staple in many of the coastal cities of the world. You do not have to be a captain of a private or military ship, a small sailboat, or a luxury cruiser to appreciate lighthouses. These stationary beacons of light save ships, save precious cargo, and—most important—save lives. The main purpose of a lighthouse is to help all watercraft navigate away from what could be a dangerous collision. Even the mightiest ships do not fare well with an unintentional grounding or a collision with a rocky cliff.

Lighthouses also serve as navigational guides. In the midst of storms, fog, or other forms of inclement weather, a lighthouse serves as a visual navigational aid. It is particularly important to highlight the necessity of a lighthouse in the midst of these storms. The darkness that comes after the sun goes down creates navigational challenges, but you can imagine how a stormy night would make safe passage extremely treacherous.

Lighthouses have an interesting history. Long before they existed, ships were guided by the fires lit at strategic points on hilltops. Lighthouses were not yet used to warn of the shore, cliffs, or reefs but functioned as markers to ports. Later fires were lit on a structure, and these evolved into a variety of lighthouse architecture.

As far back as the pharaohs of Alexandria, people were designing and using lighthouse-type structures. Other famous lighthouses with historical interest include the Tower of Hercules and England's Dover lighthouse. There are even depictions of lighthouses on coins from Alexandria, Ostia, and Laodicea. These lighthouses would have been fueled by wood or coal to keep the fires burning. As lighthouses evolved so did the purposes of their use. Captains began to depend on them as warnings to help them avoid shipping hazards. Lighthouses have served their purpose for a few millennia, but the invention of lightships added a new dimension in how lights could help make safer the busy shipping channels of our world.

Lightships may date back to the Romans. It is believed that Roman galley ships, rowed by slaves, had mast stumps with iron baskets. Fires lit in those baskets would have two basic purposes—to deter pirates and to guide ships carefully into harbor.

Lightships and their purposes evolved over time into innovative and carefully engineered vessels. In the fifteenth century Dutch lightships ventured out every night when the last fishing vessel came in. This process occurred every day. The first recorded ship was called the *Nore* and was positioned on the English coast in 1731. Lightships like the *Nore* were positioned where the water was much too deep to build any kind of permanent structure.

Over the years the duty that lightships served often placed them in harm's way. Many lightships were destroyed in hurricanes and other severe storms, including *Lightship No. 84*, a 135-foot vessel weighing 683 tons, which now lies at the bottom of New York Harbor, its two masts still poking above the surface. Because lightships helped ships navigate to safety, they often stayed out too long in storms or did not have the ability to pull out of harm's way under their own power. The main responsibility of a lightship crew was to maintain the light, although the crews on some of them were tasked with recording passing ships. Others also observed the weather and would occasionally perform rescues. But shining the light so others could safely navigate was the main task of a lightship.

— • —

Of course there are many spiritual applications to consider from lightships. For starters, as the Light of the world, Christ is our light in the midst of life's storms. When Jesus walked on earth He was a literal calmer of a storm, but who He is, is greater than what He did. Like a lightship, Christ as our light is our ever-present guide in any storm life throws our way. As the Author and Finisher of the faith, Christ stands alone as the way, He fully represents all truth, and He alone represents the fullness of life.

The purpose of a lightship is to be a constant marker. Though the wind and waves may bounce it up and down, a lightship that fulfills its purpose does not move. Likewise, Christ is our constant. He is not moved by the storms and circumstances of our lives.

Lightships also help passing ships avoid hazards. If we fix our eyes on Jesus He is sure to keep us from stumbling on the hazards of life. If we are shipwrecked, the fault is not on the guiding light but on us if we ignored the warning.

We can also trust that in the midst of the darkest storm the light of Christ does not cease to shine. He not only serves as our guide to avoid danger but is also our signal that our harbor is near. He marks the finish line where the focus of our journey should remain.

His light also thwarts the plans of pirates on the journey. His light is a protective light as well as a guiding one.

Jesus not only proclaimed that He was light but also proclaimed to us—as individuals and as His body, the church—"You are light":

You are the light of the world. A city on a hill cannot be hidden. Neither do people light a lamp and put it under a bowl. Instead they put it on its stand, and it gives light to everyone in the house. In the same way, let your light shine before men, that they may see your good deeds and praise your Father in heaven. (Matthew 5:14–16)

With His light we are given a great responsibility. Just as the lightship is moored (tied) to a buoy that helps the craft maintain a stationary position, we are moored to Christ and called to shine for His glory. One of the responsibilities we hold is to help others in their storms. We are to be a source of love, comfort, and guidance to all those facing life's storms.

God's Word instructs us that the world will know us by our love for one another. Love for one another is demonstrated when we are willing to stand firm in the midst of the storm so that others might find their way. It is also demonstrated when believers are willing to stand for God in the midst of their own personal storms and become a source of hope and inspiration to others.

Since the beginning the disciples understood that they would face trouble in order to spread the gospel. Like the police officers, firefighters, and rescue personnel who ran into the Twin Towers on 9/11, some people run into tragic situations while everyone else runs out.

— • —

Hebrews 11 has incredible insight on how God has used people over the course of history to shine for God so that the whole world would have God's light to guide them to His eternal truth.

In the midst of the greatest storms, the thickest fog, or the darkest night, those who are called by God as lightships just keep shining. They shine to bring hope. They shine to mark safe passage. They shine to ward off the pirates and thieves. They serve as beacons of the light of Christ and the light that is to come.

So be a lightship. When others face life's dark storms, arise and shine. When people feel lost and alone, shine bright. God may call you to go into harm's way, but your reward is great. We are called to Be Light, and wherever light shines darkness cannot overcome. We are called to be like the crew of the lightship, whose main task was to assure that the light stayed on.

When the people of God and the presence of God come together, then the purpose of God stands revealed.

Keep the light on!

============ Reflection ============

Shine His Light

Arise, shine, for your light has come,

    and the glory of the LORD rises upon you.—Isaiah 60:1

There are things others can borrow, but never let anyone borrow the oil designated for your lamp. Don't lend out the gifting of God's blessing!

Your anointing came with a price. You fought, suffered, and overcame for that anointing.

In Matthew 25 the wise virgins had extra oil for their lamps, the same oil the foolish tried to borrow. Today, ask God for fresh oil for your lamp so you can shine His light for all to see His glory!

26

Fire!

Our faith stands measured not by what we do when heaven falls upon us but rather by what we do when hell stands next to us.

think there might be a little "pyro" in most of us. A pyromaniac is an individual who is completely addicted to fire or to blowing things up. To be a true pyro you need to love fire, to not be able to spend a day without it.

The movie *Backdraft* gave an interesting look at the power of fires and the treacherous occupation of firefighting. At one point in the film a flame comes under a doorway and seems to have lifelike characteristics. The flame dances and contorts into a variety of shapes, and one of the characters seems to suggest that though fire is the enemy, it is also beautiful and almost magical.

Consider the illuminating benefit of fire. Fire was the very first source of light that eliminated the darkness of night for mankind. Without the torch, the candle, and other early inventions, humanity would have been unable to function effectively for almost half of every given day.

In biblical times the absence of fire was equal to the absence of light. From Genesis to Revelation there were really only two constant sources of light—the first being the sun and the other being fire in some form of a flame. The only other conceivable source of light would have been the glory of God. So without fire people were blind after dusk, and only a flame could illuminate an otherwise dark room, road, or other hidden place because the moon's light waxes and wanes.

According to Scripture, God's Word is a "lamp unto my feet, and a light unto my path" (Psalm 119:105, KJV). Consequently, God's Word is like two different ancient light fixtures. First was the lamp, which consisted of a vessel, some oil, and a burning wick. The other fixture for lighting a pathway was probably a torch, which required some fuel to burn and a structure housing the flame.

If the psalmist were writing today, what imagery might he use? Maybe God's Word would be likened to a low beam to see where I am stepping next and a high beam illuminating the road ahead? A person walking a short distance on a known path at night could have used a smaller lamp, but a torch would have been needed for lighting the way farther into unknown territory. Of course, another huge benefit of fire is that it warms. Long before we had the luxury of many modern heating mechanisms, we had crackling fires. Warming up by the fire probably dates back to the first person who lit one! A roaring fire on a cool night will warm the person sitting next to it. Once fire was brought indoors, most any shelter could be kept warm. Today, although we have heat sources at the touch of a thermostat, there is still nothing quite like putting a log in a fireplace. The fire warms, it soothes, and it makes a dwelling place feel complete.

Another obvious benefit of fire is the ability to cook food. With fire came the ability to safely cook food that in raw form caused indigestion or illness. It also made possible the delight of both flavorful and nourishing dishes! Fire also produces energy. It did not take long for human ingenuity to discover the power of fire as it pertains to engines. One of the earlier uses of steam was the powering of ships and locomotives.

Then came the use of fire in combustion engines, which changed transportation forever. For a typical automobile to have the power to move, its engine practically needs to be on fire. It is a controlled fire but a fire nonetheless. This concept soon powered airplanes and then jets, rockets, and missiles. Eventually, fire made it possible for space shuttles to rise above the earth's atmosphere.

Fire was the driving force of the industrial and motorized revolutions.

— • —

Fire is the only form of "combustive" light. A very specific mixture of elements is needed for fire, and it is important to note that there are efficient fires and inefficient ones. God is the provider of efficient fire, which is both a natural and a supernatural truth. Everything God creates is efficient, and the fire He provides for you is more than efficient. God has provided a fire that He has chosen to give and perpetually burn in the lives of all who follow Him and live according to His purpose.

Throughout the Old Testament, fire is one of the most necessary ingredients for worship. Without fire there could be no burnt sacrifices in the tabernacle or later in the temple. Yet the first mention of fire in Scripture is not related to sacrifice but came earlier in the garden of Eden. After God drove Adam and Eve out of the garden, He placed on the east side "cherubim and a flaming sword flashing back and forth to guard the way to the tree of life" (Genesis 3:24). This was not a scene of worship, and though it appears to be related to judgment, it's not that either. The cherubim with the flaming sword were not keeping Adam and Eve from something promised but were protecting them from a tree with fruit that if eaten would have caused them to live an eternal, miserable, godless life of perpetual sin. Thus, the first flame or fire in Scripture was a protective fire. It symbolized that God's presence intentionally leads God's children into His will. It was God's will for His children to be in His presence for eternity, so He determined to protect that future with fire.

Later, fire was introduced in worship at Noah's altar: "Then Noah built an altar to the LORD and, taking some of all the clean animals and clean birds, he sacrificed burnt offerings on it" (Genesis 8:20). As Noah's first act, in a world just purged from immeasurable corruption and sin, he built an altar, ignited a fire, and led his family in worship to the Lord.

In order for there to be a true act of worship in the Old Testament, something had to die and something had to be consumed. Death came by piercing, but the consumption necessitated fire.

— • —

Abraham is considered the father of faith—the very foundation of God's chosen people rested on his shoulders. Abraham knew how to build an altar, how to choose the right sacrifice, and how to offer it up to the Lord. God tested Abraham by asking him to offer his son. Abraham understood the ingredients for worship. He would have to have a knife, some wood, a fire, and a sacrifice:

> Abraham took the wood for the burnt offering and placed it on his son Isaac, and he himself carried the fire and the knife. (Genesis 22:6)

As already noted, fire cannot exist without oxygen and fuel. Abraham had dry wood, which will easily ignite and burn. Dry wood is dead. In order for us to burn for the Lord and be a light in this world, we must be that kind of fuel. We must allow God to cut away all that opposes His will, character, and ways. All the dead in us must become fuel for the fire to burn within. In a world full of darkness, He asks us to be ignited for Him.

> Isaac spoke up and said to his father Abraham, "Father?"
> "Yes, my son?" Abraham replied.
> "The fire and wood are here," Isaac said, "but where is the lamb for the burnt offering?" (verse 7)

God is a God of provision. He will never leave us empty handed. He provided Abraham with the lamb in a nearby thicket. Praise be to God that the Lamb has been provided and that the Lamb has overcome!

Another incredible instance of fire in the Old Testament occurred with Moses's encounter with the burning bush. "There the angel of the LORD appeared to him in flames of fire from within a bush. Moses saw that though the bush was on fire it did not burn up. So Moses thought, 'I will go over and see this strange sight—why the bush does not burn up'" (Exodus 3:2–3).

This scene involves a true theophany. An angel, whose true identity may have been the preincarnate Christ, appeared in flames of fire. Moses had a conversation with the angel of fire, and for the first time God's true name and God's true plan were revealed to Moses and, subsequently, to God's people. It is not coincidence that fire was a key component in this encounter. God sent Moses, and when God sends people, He empowers people.

This was not the only time fire made a grand appearance when God was about to send someone into a divine endeavor. Fire accompanied Moses throughout the deliverance of God's people. First it was the command that came from a fiery bush that sent Moses on his way. Then when Moses confronted Pharaoh and asked for the release of God's people, one of the plagues brought thunder, hail, and fire. Finally there came the greatest appearance of all: a pillar of fire led and protected the people of Israel in their deliverance. "By day the LORD went ahead of them in a pillar of cloud to guide them on their way and by night in a pillar of fire to give them light, so that they could travel by day or night. Neither the pillar of cloud by day nor the pillar of fire by night left its place in front of the people" (Exodus 13:21–22).

God is a God of motion. He moves. And the very essence of light is motion. Fire also has this in common—it, too, moves constantly. In this case a pillar of fire moved in an unusual way: it led. This pillar served as a light at night, a protector from enemies, and a symbol that God was with His people.

An interesting thing happened early on in the great march away from Egypt. This time the pillar of fire moved behind the people and stood in the gap between them and the Egyptians. Then at the very point when Israel was crossing the Red Sea on dry land, "during the last watch of the night the LORD looked down from the pillar of fire and cloud at the Egyptian army and threw it into confusion" (14:24). The Lord Himself was on the pillar of fire!

Both the Old and New Testaments, from Genesis to Revelation, reveal how God often is present in fire. However, the grandest appearance of fire, which set things in place for the future of the apostles, the church, and all who would come to know the Lord, is what happened with fire in the upper room: "Suddenly a sound like the blowing of a violent wind came from heaven and filled the whole house where they were sitting. They saw what seemed to be tongues of fire that separated and came to rest on each of them. All of them were filled with the Holy Spirit and began to speak in other tongues as the Spirit enabled them" (Acts 2:2–4).

The fire of the upper room was once again an assurance that God would be the sender of His people, would empower His people, and would continuously inhabit His people through the Holy Spirit. We can face darkness because we have His fire within us.

We can overpower darkness because of His fire within us.

We can witness with boldness because of the fire within us.

We can live empowered lives because of the fire within us.

I do believe there really is some pyro within each of us! Yet it is not the kind of pyro that likes to watch fire. We are the kind of pyro that burns for God, and we are called to light up the world with His presence.

There is no such thing as Christianity on mute. Raise your voice with truth and love.

My challenge to you today is to burn for Him and bring light to the darkness!

Reflection

Push Back the Darkness!

For you were once darkness, but now you are light in the
Lord.—Ephesians 5:8

Jesus changed the world because of who He was, what He said, and what He did: His character, His rhetoric, and His actions. Let us do likewise.

Live as children of light.

For we are the light of the world. As light, we shine on the quintessential lamp stand of truth and love.

We shine when we understand that Christianity is less about promoting the perfect and more about blessing the broken.

We illuminate our surroundings when we embrace the truth that Christianity stands measured not by the level of rhetorical eloquence but rather by the constant of loving actions.

We magnify the light empowered by the conviction that today's complacency is tomorrow's captivity.

We push back darkness when we recognize that all, in and out of the womb, carry the image of God without exception.

27

Safelight

What you say "no" to will determine
what God says "yes" to.

Any photographer who really knows the trade understands the great convenience of the digital camera. Some may say that using the film and darkroom method of traditional photographic processing creates a higher quality picture, but no one can deny that a digital camera makes it easier to retrieve the shots waiting to be framed.

When printing a photograph, you must work in a darkroom because exposure to certain light will overexpose the paper and ruin the precious photo. Photographic paper is sensitive to the blue and green colors in the light spectrum, so if the film developer wants to see what he is doing (don't we all need to see what we are doing?), he needs to use an amber or red light. This amber or red light allows one to see around the darkroom, yet not ruin the photos. This light is properly referred to as a safelight. A safelight is simply a normal light source, such as an ordinary white light bulb covered with a red or amber filter. This works because photographic paper is nearly or completely insensitive to those colors in the light spectrum.

In many ways Christ is like a safelight for humanity. Yes, He is the overpowering Light that expels darkness and declares His glory. But He is also the soft Light that loves us and waits for us to respond. Jesus tells us that He stands at the door and knocks, and if anyone hears His voice and opens the door He will come in (Revelation 3:20). Jesus will not force the door down and demand access to change your life. He is gentle and loving. He waits patiently so that He may sit and talk with you and do His work. You will not and cannot come out of failure until you know who you are in Christ and who Christ is in you.

As a carpenter Jesus knew a thing or two about a workroom. A carpenter would have need of the proper space, proper tools, a good worktable, and the working material. The Word proclaims of Christ, "He who has begun a good work in you will complete it" (Philippians 1:6, NKJV). As a master carpenter Jesus is doing the good work in you. Your job is to step into His workroom and trust that the soft light of the Master will allow Him to continue His loving and patient work.

Though this safelight concept is not discussed often, it is not a new idea. We can find evidence of God being a safelight in the Old Testament. The Lord told Elijah,

> "Go out and stand on the mountain in the presence of the LORD, for the LORD is about to pass by."
> Then a great and powerful wind tore the mountains apart and shattered the rocks before the LORD, but the LORD was not in the wind. After the wind there was an earthquake, but the LORD was not in the earthquake. After the earthquake came a fire, but the LORD was not in the fire. And after the fire came a gentle whisper. When Elijah heard it, he pulled his cloak over his face and went out and stood at the mouth of the cave. (1 Kings 19:11–13)

God was, and is, totally capable of using grand and terrifying events to show His glory and might and to get our attention. He is the God of the great winds, earthquakes, and fire. But in all the natural events that proclaimed His name, He came in the still, small voice. Could you imagine how long Elijah waited for the Lord to come? Have you ever been in a windstorm or an earthquake or witnessed a wildfire? A strong windstorm lasts for days and days.

Earthquakes can have aftershocks that occur for a long while. Wildfires can burn for months on end. God could have used any of those natural cataclysmic phenomena to approach Elijah, but He waited until all was still to speak to Elijah in a quiet way, like a loving Father or best friend. How great is it that the God of the universe, capable of thunderous sounds and earthshaking tempests, would be so gentle and personal with us as to use a still, small voice?

When we look at salvation, it seems like a big bang exposure to the light and goodness of Christ, and properly so. The moment of salvation is the defining moment of one's life. But what happens after the big bang light is over? That is where the safelight glow of sanctification comes in. Sanctification is what happens after salvation. It is the slow and continuous transformation of the old self to become more and more like Christ, with the help of the Holy Spirit. Here is where the Romans 12:2 "processing" takes effect. Your mind is being renewed and you are being transformed by the work of the Holy Spirit in a workroom illuminated by the loving safelight of Christ.

Sanctification is the ongoing part of salvation. It will never cease until the day you are with Christ in glory. Just like the safelight slowly but surely exposes photographic film, sanctification slowly but surely makes us new. It is described as "now and not yet."

Sanctification is not solely the work of the Holy Spirit; we must do our part to respond to the safelight He provides. If God is calling us to change our ways and we do not respond, sanctification cannot take place. We must do our part so that He can do His. When we submit to His safelight and His workroom, we allow Him to bring His plan for us into fruition. The safelight of the Holy Spirit transforms us to be a safelight for others, inviting them with gentleness to come into relationship with the One who transformed and is transforming us.

— • —

God calls us to be the light of this world. He tells us to let our light shine before others so they can see our good deeds and bring glory to Him (Matthew

5:14–16). Being a light in this world means allowing our actions to stand out in righteousness among the darkness that surrounds us. These actions include, but are not limited to, honest intentions, good deeds, and witnessing to others about the gospel.

When they read this scripture many people imagine a spotlight or a great lamp that glows brightly and immediately affects everything it touches. God calls us many times to be a bright light, but more often than not, He invites us to be a safelight. Some people are like photographic paper living in their lonely darkrooms of life, being nearly or completely insensitive to the presence of God. Being a safelight to these people means that we are called into the darkrooms of their lives to expose them to God in a real way—a gradual exposing of the presence of God.

Being a safelight requires faith and perseverance. Much like a safelight takes time to process a photo, it takes time for some people to realize they are being affected by God's presence. Results are not quickly noted. Most of the time safelights don't even know they are witnessing with their actions. We must be careful not to intend that all our actions will affect people's lives. We need just to work willingly at whatever we do, as though we are working for the Lord rather than for people (see Colossians 3:23). We must not get carried away. Safelights do not set out to change things; they just do.

Being a safelight is not just witnessing; it is living an example. It means not only taking time to affect those around us but also being that steadfast, unchanging amber glow. Our righteousness has to be evident in all aspects of our lives.

Some people recall incredible stories of witnessing, when after a sentence or two someone repented and gave her life to Christ. This person's life changed immediately, and she went home and her whole family was saved—all because of one witness, one time! These stories are the ones preachers tell in their sermons and then end with a bold challenge. Nothing is wrong with these stories; they are all true, and it is a beautiful thing that happens by the grace of God. Even so, they represent only a fraction of the stories of coming to salvation.

Once, a Korean girl came to America on what would be a life-transforming adventure. As a student in California, her intention was merely to receive her high-school diploma and attend a great university. She lived in the same Christian household for all four years of her high-school career. Her host family grew to love her and brought her to church every Sunday. They tried many times to talk to her about God and tell her of Jesus's sacrifice, but the girl was never interested. She evaded all conversation and never said a word about her beliefs.

For four years she went to church with her host family and was unfazed by the "Jesus talk." Finally her time with the host family was coming to an end as graduation drew ever near. It was her last Sunday going to church with her host family. She sat in her usual place. The pastor preached a regular sermon. It was not flashy or particularly important to the congregation. All of a sudden, the girl began to cry. Tears rolled down her face as she went to the altar and accepted Jesus as her Lord and Savior. Her host family praised the Lord!

Overjoyed, and a little puzzled, the girl's host family asked her what had caused her to feel the need for salvation all of a sudden: Was it what the pastor said or something that had happened to her? She looked at them and said that it was them. They never had ceased showing her God's love. Ultimately, she wanted to be like them.

If it wasn't for the safelight actions of the entire host family, the girl might never have accepted Christ. It was their steadfast love that brought her to be aware of God and His love for her. Their steady love changed her life.

— • —

We are called to Be Light as He is light. At times this calling is to be a safelight as He is a safelight. Not a compromised light, not a light that changes with the social issues of our times, but a true, loving, inviting light for Christ.

It takes faith to move a mountain, courage to climb a mountain, vision to conquer a mountain, and wisdom to move around a mountain.

It's time to do something.

Is God calling you to be a safelight today?

The Ordinary Becomes Extraordinary in the Presence of God!

The angel of the LORD appeared to him and said, "Mighty hero, the LORD is with you!"—Judges 6:12, NLT

Wait, wait! God began by calling Gideon a mighty hero, a warrior?

Imagine Gideon's face. *Me? You talking to me? I'm threshing wheat hiding from the bad guys and You call me what?*

God didn't say he "will one day be." Rather, He engaged a present-tense descriptor. In other words, *you* are a mighty hero!

28

The Milky Way

You may not receive it when you expect it, but once you get it, it will be bigger than you expected!

Have you ever stopped to think about where you are? This may seem to be a very simple question, but it is actually extremely complex. The vastness of our universe is truly incomprehensible. There is only so much of our universe that scientists can see, and beyond that, it is unknown.

So where are you? Our home, Earth, is located in our solar system, and our solar system is located in the spiral of the Milky Way galaxy called the Orion Arm. The Milky Way galaxy is in a small group of galaxies called the Local Group. The Local Group is in the Laniakea Supercluster, which is a massive group of galaxies held together by gravity.

Just to put this in perspective, the Local Group has twenty bright galaxies and thirty galaxies in total. There are other known superclusters in our observable universe, but scientists believe there can be up to ten million of these clusters of galaxies. *Laniakea* is a Hawaiian word that means "immeasurable heavens." Believe it or not, our Milky Way galaxy is the brightest galaxy in the Laniakea Supercluster, and Earth is an infinitesimal speck in this neighborhood.

We who live on Earth are located about halfway between the edge and the center of the Milky Way, about twenty to twenty-five thousand light-years between the center and the edge. A light-year is the distance light travels in one year. This is so interesting because some stars we see are actually light that has taken years to reach our planet. To have an idea of how big the Milky Way is, let us look at how long it would take to make a trip across our neighborhood. One light-year is equivalent to 5.88 trillion miles (5,878,499,810,000 miles). If you were to travel at 511 miles per hour, which is the average cruising speed of a 737 airliner, it would take about 11.5 billion hours. This translates to 1.3 million years, just to go the distance of one light-year!

The Milky Way from end to end is about one hundred thousand light-years. Again, *about* is used because nothing is absolute. So if you were on a flight going the cruising speed of a Boeing 737, it would take roughly 131 trillion years to travel from one side to the other. If you were somehow able to defy the laws of physics and travel at the speed of light, it would still take about one hundred thousand years. This is how vast our Milky Way is!

We are in the brightest galaxy and just happen to be the only planet known to man with life on it. Now you know exactly where you are! Let us take a closer look at our beautiful neighborhood known as the Milky Way. The ancient Romans called our galaxy *via lacteal,* which means "road of milk." They got this idea from the Greeks, who called it *galaxias kyklos,* which translates as "milky circle." It is quite obvious why they called it this, as we can see a band of "milky" light that streams beautifully across the night sky.

Sometimes the Milky Way may be hard to see, due to light pollution from city lights, as it is not that bright. But for those in the parts of the world who have the opportunity to see our wonderful home in the stars, it is quite a breathtaking sight.

There are an estimated 200 to 400 billion stars in our galaxy. What we see is the brightness of all these stars in our galaxy put together. This creates the band of faint white light arcing across the sky, which is actually the Milky Way on its side. All the stars we can see with our naked eye are in the Milky Way, but what we see as the milky light is a blur of stars.

This is an amazing thing to consider, all these lights coming together to form something beautiful that we can see. How powerful this is that large stars many light-years away would come together and form something beautiful that we can admire. Our home in the universe is beautiful and full of light. How great is our God who would place us in this beautiful "neighborhood" for us to admire His majesty.

Why here? Why is this our home in this huge universe? Why would a God so great place us among these beautiful stars? Perhaps these lights that surround us are intended to point us to Him. These lights and stars come together at night, many light-years apart, and display to us something magnificent. How amazing is this that this band of milky light would span our night sky and remind us of God's power.

He made the universe, He made the Milky Way, He made our solar system, He made Earth, and He made us. We are nothing compared to the size of His vast creation. Still, He loves us so much that His creation gives us something to look up to at night and reflect on. The God who crafted our home, the Milky Way galaxy, also crafted you. God's Word reminds us that "every good and perfect gift is from above, coming down from the Father of the heavenly lights, who does not change like shifting shadows" (James 1:17).

The word *lights* used in James 1:17 is also used in Genesis 1:14. It says, "And God said, 'Let there be *lights* in the vault of the sky to separate the day from the night, and let them serve as signs to mark sacred times, and days and years'" (NIV, 2011). God spoke the universe into being. He merely breathed, and our Milky Way was formed.

The stars and the heavens are there for us, to tell time and mark "sacred times." How powerful is our wonderful Father? He gives us the ability to study and fathom how immense our galaxy is: one hundred thousand light-years, full of stars, brought together to make the Milky Way. Our God did this. The stars give us something to look up to in amazement and realize the awe-inspiring power of the Father of lights.

It is easy to appreciate the name given to the Milky Way, this celestial wonder, in light of Scripture. The heavens not only declare the beauty, majesty, and handiwork of the Lord, but they also can lead people to truth. Why are we here? What is our purpose?

God gave you a gift, a dream, a miracle, a promise, and it seems like it's gone? It's not gone; it's coming back to you! But this time it's coming back protected, provided for, and promoted. Whatever you placed in God's hands, when you see it again, when you hold it in your arms, it will be greater than you ever expected!

Jesus said, "I am the way, the truth, and the life" (John 14:6, NKJV). Wait! Why does it begin with *way*? We know that His Word proclaims that there is only one way to salvation. There is only one way to the Father. We know that His disciples first called their new ministry the Way. Their life's work, which literally cost them their lives, was spent preparing the way of the Lord. They were called to be the first lights, lights that would light up the way.

Jesus is the living Word. "In the beginning was the Word, and the Word was with God, and the Word was God" (John 1:1). As stated in earlier chapters, Scripture proclaims, "Thy Word is a lamp unto my feet, and a light unto my path" (Psalm 119:105, KJV). Jesus, the living Word, showed us the path we are to take, a path for both a great life and an eternity with Him. The written Word also is an illuminated instruction manual pointing the way. Yet there are many more ingredients to this system of lights.

Jesus calls all of us to be lights for the world. When we allow God to light our own individual light, we can accomplish amazing things. What happens when many lights cluster together? We become a pathway leading to a true land flowing with milk and honey. The Milky Way is so vast, so large one must stand in awe. Yet when we come together as God's light, we create an equally vast array of lights that can lead a broken world to a healing Savior. From the dimension of the spirit, imagine how saints shine. We shine along our way, we shine to light the way, and we shine to point to the way.

To truly appreciate the Milky Way, you have to remove yourself from the heavily populated parts of our world. Many people find God when they leave the minutiae of life and escape to a place where they can see clearly. This world throws so many distractions along our journey. This world has confused priorities, with its twisting of truth and deceptive spirits. Yet when the lights shine together, those who seek Christ are aided by those who have found Him.

Abraham is the father of faith and the father of the promise. When God gave Abraham an idea about the promise, He used the stars as a measuring point. It seems like a wonderful and beautiful thing to point out, but it has taken thousands of years to fully comprehend the expanse of the promise given to Abraham, who represented the first of God's covenant people.

Abraham was told to think about the sky. The stars were a grand companion for Abraham. People who raised sheep and other livestock depended on stars to guide them in the evening. It must have taken Abraham's breath away when the angel of the Lord proclaimed that his descendants would be as numerous as the stars. Abraham would have seen the Milky Way, and if he would have understood the number of stars in just that one cluster, the promise would have overwhelmed him all the more.

Jesus, too, inherited an immeasurable amount of children—us. Not only are we as numerous as the stars, but we are also lights: lights of the way, lights that point to the way, and lights that lead the way.

Be that light today.

Step into the Promise

> But if we walk in the light, as he is in the light, we have
> fellowship with one another, and the blood of Jesus, his
> Son, purifies us from all sin.—1 John 1:7

The generation of Israelites who made it to the promised land was not the generation that left Egypt but rather the generation born in the wilderness.

Stop for a moment and get this! The generation that was born in Egypt did not make it to the land of milk and honey. But rather it was a generation born in the wilderness, born in the hard place, born in the dry place, born in the place where water came out of rocks and manna fell from heaven.

In other words, those who left Egypt complained. They were slaves who received their provisions from their masters. They complained on occasion, "Let's go back to Egypt, where at least we had good food."

The generation born in the wilderness had no masters. They had no plan B. They had God, *only God.* If God stopped the manna, they would all die.

Which generation will step into the promise? The generation that depends solely on God.

Who will step into the promise? The person who says *only* God.

My strength is God.

My shield is God.

My salvation is God.

God is my provider.

God is my protector.

God is not a thing in my life. He is my everything.

So if you have come out of the wilderness, out of the desert of despair, out of a place where there's only God, then you qualify! Step into the promise! You are a child of the wilderness, born in the hard place, dependent only on God!

29

The Church Is the Light

We are not Google, Ford, Microsoft, or even Starbucks. We are the church of Jesus Christ, and the gates of hell shall not prevail against us!

When God created all that we see and all that we cannot see, He simply declared, "Let there be." All that we know to be true begins with His declaration. He said, "Let there be light," and there was light. He said, "Let there be an expanse between the waters," and it was so. He said, "Let the water teem with living creatures . . . [and] the land produce living creatures," and so they did (Genesis 1:3, 6, 20, 24).

It was the disciple Peter who uttered the words "you are the one, the messiah, the Christ" (see Matthew 16:16). It was his declaration that provoked Christ to declare that there would be a church, built on the truth of Peter's declaration, and that the gates of hell would not prevail against it. In essence Jesus said, "Let there be a church, the *ekklesia*," and so there was.

Everything God created declares His glory. God's glory and God's light are synonymous; thus all that God creates reveals His light. When God builds His church He builds it to reveal, possess, and declare His light. We hold this faith, the faith that His light is ours and is our clear priority.

Our one faith is not like any other faith. Our faith is transparent, transcendent, and transformational. Our faith teaches us to cross over obstacles, to shout down walls, to break through crowds, and to walk on water in the midst of life's storms. Our faith enables us to survive the fires of life and overcome the den of lions. Our faith silences the serpent and outwits the fox. Our faith empowers us to see the invisible, embrace the impossible, and hope for the incredible.

It is this one faith, one Lord, and one mission that empowers us to break through the minutiae of relativism, compromise, and comfortable Christianity and engage in one touch—the touch of Christ that gives us power from His glorious light and that can and will change the world. In essence we touch Him and He empowers us to touch the world.

In Mark 5 Jesus was asked by Jairus, a synagogue leader, to come with him and heal his daughter. While Jesus was on His way, a woman who had been bleeding for twelve years reached out and touched Him. She had suffered greatly. It is probable that she had not experienced human touch for twelve long years, because she would have been considered ceremonially unclean. She had tried doctors and probably other remedies, but instead of getting better, she'd gotten worse. Then she heard about Jesus and, coming through the crowd, reached out and touched His cloak.

We are called to one faith, one mission, one hope, one light, and one touch. The church is called to bring people to faith, to follow His mission, to spread His hope, and to be His light so that others can experience that touch of the Master. The church must know who Christ is in order for the world to know who Christ is. He is the Son of the living God.

Through the church God has the ability to heal one generation and touch the next generation. We live in a time when the world is sick and dying, stricken by sin, where moral relativism, immorality, and spiritual apathy are commonplace. Yet in the midst of this unprecedented spiritual pandemic, there exists good news. Jesus still saves, Jesus still delivers, Jesus still heals, and Jesus is coming again.

The woman with the issue of blood touched Jesus before Jesus touched the little girl. God is a God of order, and this was not a coincidental timing but one that shows great insight into God's plan. The answer lies in this narrative. Instead of waiting for God to touch the next generation, today's generation must reach out and touch Him.

The law of physics dictates that two objects cannot occupy the same space. Your past cannot occupy your future. Your faith cannot share space with fear, holiness cannot share space with sin, the prophetic cannot share space with the pathetic, and light cannot share space with darkness.

Ephesians 4:5 says we have "one Lord, one faith, one baptism." I believe the church of the living God is also just one touch away from a new transformation. We are one touch away from an awakening that will heal one generation and save the next generation. God is not done with His church yet. He who has begun a good work is not finished! Either we can be the generation of the church that is referred to as the generation of Facebook, Twitter, and Instagram, or history will say that ours was the generation that touched God. The angst of the church comes from the question of whether or not the next generation will be able to be a light of Christ and a light for Christ. Like the woman with the issue of blood, we must "go through to get to." We must go through a season of storms to get to our season of peace. We must go through a season of want to get to our season of plenty. Sometimes we go through a season of darkness to get to our season of light.

For the church to function fully as the light of the world, we must see ourselves *as* the church. She will shine only as brightly as we do. We are called as the church of the living God to touch the cloak of the Master and lead others to the light of the Master. Jesus is the Light of the world, and He calls us to shine as His light in our world.

You are the salt of the earth; but if the salt has become tasteless, how can
it be made salty again? It is no longer good for anything, except to be
thrown out and trampled under foot by men.

You are the light of the world. A city set on a hill cannot be hidden;

nor does anyone light a lamp and put it under a basket, but on the lampstand, and it gives light to all who are in the house. (Matthew 5:13–15, NASB)

— • —

The church is called to be a shining city on a hill. I have seen my share of cities at night. When you fly over cities, you can quickly observe their size by the spread of the lights. From the air you can sometimes observe the wealth and prestige of the city from the congestion and dynamic displays of lights, as low as the street and as high as the tallest skyscraper.

From ground level, however, it is difficult to see or appreciate a city in the evening unless it is set on a hill. When a city has been built at a higher elevation, it shines through miles of darkness. For the commuter coming home it becomes the hope that the journey is nearing an end. To a family who is tired, it is the hope that soon their heads will rest on comfortable hotel pillows. To the hungry traveler it represents the abundant cuisine offered by any given city. The light of that city truly demonstrates the hope of the city, the offerings of the city, and the shelter of the city.

There is a definite, purposeful rationale to the comparison made between the church and a city on a hill. Zion was to "shine" because her "light has come" (Isaiah 60:1). The Gentiles were to come to her light (see verse 3). Her mission as the enlightener of the world was symbolized in the ornamentations of her priesthood.

Today, the church stands as a representative of the people of God. The church is not only the body of Christ but also the people of Christ. These citizens of Christ's kingdom together can light up a city, light up a nation, and be a light to the world.

The apostle Paul, under the inspiration of the Holy Spirit, gave us a clear picture of the practice, purpose, and place of the church:

To make plain to everyone the administration of this mystery, which
for ages past was kept hidden in God, who created all things. His intent
was that now, through the church, the manifold wisdom of God should
be made known to the rulers and authorities in the heavenly realms,
according to his eternal purpose which he accomplished in Christ Jesus
our Lord. In him and through faith in him we may approach God with
freedom and confidence. (Ephesians 3:9–12)

Christ, who is the Light of the world, is the Head of the church. The
church, being His body, is the instrument through which His glory is to be
manifested to the world to make all people see. The church brings glory to God
by revealing His glory to all through its reproduction of the life and light of
Christ.

The Holy Spirit did not come down so we can stay seated singing, "Kum-
baya, my Lord." It's time to go beyond asking God to come down. It's time for
the church to stand up!

— • —

As individuals we are called to shine our light, but when we do so in the heavenly community of Christ's church, our light combines into an influencing
agent. The light of the church stands bright in a dark world. She is an empowered church, a church that Christ has built and continues to build. And the
gates of hell cannot prevail against her.

His church exposes and exorcises the Enemy and his schemes. The church
illuminates and teaches the Word to inspire the believer and invite the lost. The
church comes together to worship, to fellowship, and to disciple, but it goes out
to witness, to serve, to transform, and to shine His light seven days a week.

We close this day with blessings intended to remind us that we are called
to have God shine on us so that we, in turn, can shine for Him—to Be Light.

The LORD bless you
    and keep you;
the LORD make his face shine upon you
    and be gracious to you;
the LORD turn his face toward you
    and give you peace. (Numbers 6:24–26)

Restore us, O LORD God Almighty;
    make your face shine upon us,
    that we may be saved. (Psalm 80:19)

For God, who said, "Let light shine out of darkness," made his light shine in our hearts to give us the light of the knowledge of the glory of God in the face of Christ. (2 Corinthians 4:6)

=== Reflection ===

A Critical Answer

The LORD is my light and my salvation—

    whom shall I fear?

The LORD is the stronghold of my life—

    of whom shall I be afraid?—Psalm 27:1

We must answer with clarity, conviction, and courage that we are the light of the world!

When you accept Jesus and receive Him in your life, you become a bona fide member of the "no weapon formed against me" overcomers' club! The "yes" of our heavenly Father is more powerful than the "no" of this world.

It takes conviction to repent,

Courage to speak truth,

Holiness to see God,

Faith to move mountains,

And love to change the world!

To Be Light and Shine Forever

Be holy, be filled, be one, Be Light,
and change the world!

Over the course of our thirty encounters, I hope you have been challenged. My hope is that you have reflected on the many aspects of living in God's light and Being Light. As discussed earlier, there are really two core principles driving my topic. The first is that *God is light,* and the second is that wherever light and darkness come into contact, *light always wins.*

There is a fantastic Old Testament story that illustrates these principles:

> After the Philistines had captured the ark of God, they took it from
> Ebenezer to Ashdod. Then they carried the ark into Dagon's temple
> and set it beside Dagon. When the people of Ashdod rose early the
> next day, there was Dagon, fallen on his face on the ground before the
> ark of the LORD! They took Dagon and put him back in his place. But
> the following morning when they rose, there was Dagon, fallen on his
> face on the ground before the ark of the LORD! His head and hands
> had been broken off and were lying on the threshold; only his body
> remained. That is why to this day neither the priests of Dagon nor
> any others who enter Dagon's temple at Ashdod step on the threshold.
> (1 Samuel 5:1–5)

This story illustrates what happens when light and darkness convene. Because light always overtakes darkness, those of us in the light are called to obliterate darkness by shining perpetually for God. Two times the statue of Dagon was found lying on the ground, and soon the people who worshiped Dagon began to face all kinds of calamity. In fact, everywhere the ark went that wasn't supportive of the people of God, calamity occurred. God intended for His presence to be with His people. His light can shine only with people of His light.

So let us reflect on what we have read for the last twenty-nine days. First we set the tone for this book by being reminded of two overarching biblical themes: light fills our universe, and darkness always threatens. We have a truth that has been declared about us that helps solve the riddle of existence as it gives definition and purpose: We are the light of the world. There is an inextinguishable light within each of us, a light that can penetrate and eliminate even the darkest places.

God's Word declares, "The darkness has not overcome it" (John 1:5, NIV, 2011). There is an enduring promise and hope in that statement. Light has and will continue to overcome darkness. No matter our circumstances, no matter how bleak the future may appear, we will stand in the knowledge that we are the light of the world, and the light in us will overcome the darkness so that we can shine the light of truth in our world.

As the light of the world we reflect light, but we are more than just mirrors. We reflect the light of God, but we also must absorb the light of His presence and teaching so that we can emit a light that is truly ours and not just a surface reflection of faith.

A natural-world example is photosynthesis, which is a complex phenomenon and is more than plants simply reflecting the light of the sun. Plants must absorb sunlight and synthesize it before giving off oxygen, which is a nutrient for other life forms. In the same way, we must learn to absorb all the light God has for us and not just reflect it but reflect some, retain some, and emit some.

Nothing is more certain to increase our internal light and temperature than setting time aside each day to focus on God. Like nuclear colliders that use completely impermeable materials to shut out all external objects so that fusion will occur internally and produce power, we must have a time each day when we shut out the distractions of life that impede the creation of a spiritual fusion of our souls to God that will produce a similar power in us. Just as daily physical exercise produces a healthy body, daily spiritual exercises produce an internal "heat" in us that is caused by the light of truth that comes only from God.

We must strive to be more like God so that we can be used as His perfectly functioning mirror of truth to others. We must be those who seek out the broken ones, the forgotten and hurting ones, the physically and spiritually impoverished ones, the ones imprisoned by lies of imperfect mirrors, and we must hold up the eternal image of God, whose light shines through us to bring healing and restoration. We are the light of the world, so our words of gentle affirmation must replace the words of hatred and pain that have marred many lives. Our actions will help others see that they can walk in the light of newness.

Like a prism when light passes through it, we reveal the full color spectrum. We are called to be the light of the world, but that does not mean that we people of faith are uniform, monochromatic, or one dimensional. It is our high calling indeed to be instruments through which God reveals the various "wavelengths" that represent Him. The light of God may appear to be a single beam of white light, but when it passes through the prisms of His people, its full complexity and beauty are revealed.

One of the features of the light of God is that it reveals our shortcomings. Just as sunlight reveals particles in the atmosphere, God's light exposes the "pollution" in our lives. As difficult as it is to have our sins revealed by God's light, His light is meant to bring us to a new awareness of our shortcomings as we work diligently to cleanse ourselves of unrighteous thoughts and actions that separate us from God.

When we just glimpse the brightest, hottest objects, like the sun or a pure beam of light, we can close our eyes, but the bright image remains. If we commit to seeking God above all things, He will transform us into objects that glow so hot and bright that after others encounter us and walk away, the "bright image" of God's love will remain with them.

Since we are the light of the world, we should be able to emulate the unity displayed by a laser that gives it such power. The first parallel that comes to mind relates to the fact that laser light is all on the same wavelength. To develop laser-light qualities, we must begin by unifying our hearts, minds, and lives to God. God created us in His image and He is light, so we bear that same imprint. If we can get on God's wavelength, we will surely experience the coherence and direction that a laser has.

Aligning our light's wavelength with the Lord's is predicated on our desire to be like Him. We must hate sin the way God does, knowing that sin always keeps us from being on the same wavelength as God. Being one with the Lord and joining Him in the pure light of salvation requires everything from us. We are one with Him when we are hidden in Him, away from the darkness of sin and selfishness.

Because we are the light of the world, our mission is to pierce the darkness with the light of Christ: Christ the Messiah; Christ the Conqueror; Christ the Son of Man; Christ the Son of God; Christ the Way, the Truth, and the Life; the Resurrection and the Life; the true Vine; the good Shepherd; the Alpha and the Omega; the Author and Finisher of our faith; the One who changed water into wine, sinners into saints, and mourning into dancing. Christ, the Hope of glory!

We are the clay jars of Gideon's story and the image of clay jars in Paul's letter to the Corinthian believers: "We now have this light shining in our hearts, but we ourselves are like fragile clay jars containing this great treasure. This makes it clear that our great power is from God, not from ourselves" (2 Corinthians 4:7, NLT).

Just as in Gideon's story, the great power will come from God and not from us. We are called fragile clay jars, but in the hands of a powerful God, we are weapons for victory against tremendous, Midian-sized odds.

The light that Christ wants to give us is eternal. His light is not subject to the decay that is an inherent part of our daily lives. It gives truth. It makes us good. This is the light of the world that we must seek so that each day is a living testament of worship to our God. A life guided by intentional, ongoing sacrifice in worship will never be described as a half-life Christianity.

The light that God has given us can never be obsolete. There is no more efficient or powerful version to come in the future. It is the transcendent, eternal light that brings hope to the hopeless and lights a way for the lost. It is that beacon on the rocky shore that announces danger and the laser that intercepts weapons that are meant to harm us.

— • —

The Bible says that "Satan disguises himself as an angel of light" (2 Corinthians 11:14, NLT). The deceptive light of the Enemy makes it all the more critical for us to be the bioluminescent light that guides people to God. We are that light, the light of the world. If bioluminescent creatures need oxygen, a luciferin, and a luciferase to shine, we need these three ingredients: the Spirit of God, a willing heart, and the determination to bring His light to the oceans of darkness around us.

Because we are called to be the light of the world, we must know light in all its forms. Faith involves spiritual components of our lives, and it can sometimes be explosive and even destructive. In our zealousness to share the truth and power of God's love, we can sometimes overwhelm others with a sudden explosion of ideas that are foreign to them.

The power and beauty of light lead many to misidentify the source of light and begin confusing the light with other things, including the light giver, God. The Bible has many references to a heavenly or celestial light. Among them is Paul's description in his first letter to Timothy, when he wrote about the "Lord of lords, who alone is immortal and who lives in unapproachable light, whom no one has seen or can see" (6:15–16). The brightest light has not yet shone into this world. It will come when Christ returns, but until that day, He is counting on us, poor vessels who lack His magnetic power, to shine brightly for all to see.

We are the light of the world, and we aspire to the power of magnetars as we cling to the One who made them, and us, to shine for His glory.

Light and darkness cannot coexist. When light enters the mind, darkness is overtaken. The remedy for dark thoughts is not merely positive thinking; it is the introduction of God's holy light into the mind so that mental patterns are transformed.

When light is introduced it does not slowly shine; it is immediate. Light exposes and expels darkness, but the damage of darkness, its habits, its scars, and its evasiveness slowly begin to give way to a new template and a new standard for thinking. Christ becomes a new mental pacesetter for those who have surrendered their souls to Him who is light so that the path to holiness is pursued.

When the light of each new day comes (dawn, aurora), the wind (boreas) of the Holy Spirit should produce in us the spectacular effect of the northern lights. This means that God does not just dance over you, but when He overtakes your life He is dancing within you. You become a walking, talking northern light. Your mission is to bring joy to those around you because of the joy within you, to bring light to those around you because of the light within you, and to be both a recipient and a conduit of God's glory in this world.

We have learned that in the midst of the most chaotic shaking we might ever experience, God's glory is evident. Even the most incredible personal earthquake you are going through or have experienced can produce some of the most brilliant light in your life. What you think has come to destroy you has come to produce light in you.

With His light we are given a great responsibility. Like the lightship that was moored (tied) to a buoy to maintain a stationary position, we are moored to Christ and called to shine for His glory. One of the responsibilities we hold is to help others in their storms. We are to be sources of love, comfort, and guidance to all those facing life's storms.

We not only leave darkness but are also engaged in a war with darkness—a war that feels very much one dimensional but that according to Scripture is actually multidimensional. In other words, the war or the struggle we are engaged in here is mirrored in heavenly places. The light produced by spiritual collisions that involve us also produces light and has spiritual consequences in heavenly realms. This means that every time we are under spiritual attack, what we see manifested on earth is dwarfed in comparison to what is manifesting in the heavens.

Finally, we learned that as individuals we are called to shine our light, but when we do so in the heavenly community of Christ's church, our many points of light combine into an influencing agent. The light of the church stands bright in a dark world. She is an empowered church, a church that Christ has built and continues to build. And the gates of hell cannot prevail against her.

— • —

The time has come for us to shine continuously. We can ill afford to be extinguished by the trappings of this world. When we see our role and place in the kingdom, we will shine like ever-burning lamps.

Interestingly, there are a number of examples of such unquenchable lamps—in antiquity and in more modern times—from all parts of the world, flames burning continuously without fuel on several continents.[1]

- Plutarch wrote of a lamp that burned over the door of a temple to Jupiter Ammon. The priests reported it had burned for centuries without a fuel source.
- Saint Augustine described a perpetual lamp in a temple in Egypt sacred to Venus, which nothing could extinguish. Augustine thought it was the devil's work.
- During emperor Justinian's reign, an inextinguishable lamp was found at Edessa (Antioch) in a niche over the city gate. A date on the lamp proved it had been burning for more than five hundred years.

- In England during the Middle Ages, a lamp was found that had reportedly burned since the third century at the tomb believed to be of the father of Constantine the Great.
- The Lantern of Pallas was discovered near Rome in 1401 in the sepulcher of Pallas, son of Evander, immortalized by Virgil in his *Æneid*. The lamp supposedly had burned for more than two thousand years.
- In 1550 on an island in the Bay of Naples, a burning lamp was found in a marble vault. The light had been set there before the Christian era.
- In our own time, at a fire-department station in Livermore, California, the Centennial Light—the longest burning light bulb in history—is now in its 114th year (in 2015) of illumination and has burned for one million hours.[2]

— • —

It is now time to shine continuously until we leave this life and our light joins the Light Giver forever. We who are in Christ will outshine these relics because the living, everlasting God is our fuel. There is but one thing left to do: Be Light!

The New Day

For God, who said, "Let light shine out of darkness,"
made his light shine in our hearts to give us the light of
the knowledge of the glory of God in the face of Christ.
—2 Corinthians 4:6

Let me tell you about the new day coming.

In the morning . . .

His mercies are new!

Great is His faithfulness; His mercies begin afresh each morning.

Joy arrives!

For His anger is but for a moment, and His favor is for a lifetime.

Weeping may tarry for the night, but joy comes with the morning.

The prophetic arises!

Today, speak over your house, marriage, money, circumstances, and faith, and say,

"It's morning! It's a new day!"

Throughout Scripture, the most successful men and women have stood up and made outrageous declarations and requests that came to pass:

Moses: "Show me Your glory."

Caleb: "Give me that mountain."

Elisha: "I want a double portion."

Hezekiah: "Give me more years."

Jabez: "Bless me indeed. Enlarge my territory."

And for all of them the answer: "Request granted!"

Why? Because when you believe God for the impossible, you begin to walk in the incredible!

Acknowledgments

Dr. Carlos Campo, my fellow Trekkie and partner in grace, thank you. Your collaboration and participation in the super-intense strategy session unleashed heaven. I'm eternally grateful.

Dr. Nick Garza, after close to twenty-five years running together, I find your brilliance continues to change lives. And to think you are just getting started.

My beautiful wife, Eva, and my children, Yvonne, Nathan, and Lauren. You inspire me.

My parents, Sam and Elizabeth, sisters and friends. For you.

Finally, this message was first preached behind the podium of the most beautiful church and the greatest congregation—New Season in Sacramento. Your Pastor loves you.

Notes

Chapter 1: Be Light!

1. Susan Welch, "Teen who nearly drowned at Lake Sainte Louise heads home," *St. Louis Post-Dispatch,* February 5, 2015, www.stltoday.com /lifestyles/health-med-fit/teen-who-nearly-drowned-at-lake-sainte -louise-heads-home/article_43db7316-908b-5805-86e5-01fdc8eee 581.html.

Chapter 2: Knowing Light

1. Charles Q. Choi, "Earth's Sun: Facts About the Sun's Age, Size and History," Space.com, November 20, 2014, www.space.com /58-the-sun-formation-facts-and-characteristics.html. See also Jeffrey M. Walch, et al, "The effect of sunlight on postoperative analgesic medication use: a prospective study of patients undergoing spinal surgery," Psychosomatic Medicine 67, no. 1 (January/February 2005):156–63, http://citeseerx.ist.psu.edu/viewdoc/download?doi =10.1.1.537.947&rep=rep1&type=pdf.

2. David Crouch, "Swedish school sheds light on dark days of winter," *The Guardian,* January 24, 2015, www.theguardian.com/world/2015 /jan/24/swedish-school-light-dark-days-winter.

3. Cathy Lynn Grossman, "A Beacon of Hope: The Importance of Light in Religion," *USA Weekend,* December 22, 2011, www.usaweekend .com/article/20111223/HOME02/312230011/A-beacon-hope -importance-light-religion.

4. "Albedo," Wikipedia, https://en.wikipedia.org/wiki/Albedo.

5. 1 John 1:7, KJV

Chapter 3: Overcoming Darkness

1. Terry Pratchett, *Reaper Man* (New York: Harper Collins, 2013), 311.
2. Francesca Gino, "What Darkness Does to the Mind," *The Atlantic*, June 13, 2013, www.theatlantic.com/health/archive/2013/06/what-darkness-does-to-the-mind/276578/.
3. Office of the Clark County Prosecuting Attorney, Indiana, "Robert Wesley Knighton," www.clarkprosecutor.org/html/death/US/knighton855.htm.

Chapter 4: We Emit What We Absorb

1. John 3:30, NRSVCE

Chapter 5: Increasing Our Internal Temperature

1. L. Terry Clausing, "Emissivity: Understand the Difference Between Apparent, Actual IR Temps," Reliable Plant, www.reliableplant.com/Read/14134/emissivity-underst-difference-between-apparent,-actual-ir-temps.
2. Gary Neal Hansen, *Kneeling with Giants: Learning to Pray with History's Best Teachers* (Downers Grove, IL: InterVarsity, 2012), 16.
3. Hansen, *Kneeling with Giants*, 5.
4. Marianne Bernard, "Dying with Faith," *God's Promises Are Real* blog, November 19, 2008, http://mvbernard.com/tag/gods-calm-assurance-in-all-things/.

Chapter 6: The Law of Reflection

1. Chanel Parks, "78 Percent of Women Spend an Hour a Day on Their Appearance, Study Says," *The Huffington Post*, February 24, 2014, www.huffingtonpost.com/2014/02/24/women-daily-appearance-study_n_4847848.html.
2. "Mirror," Wikipedia, https://en.wikipedia.org/wiki/Mirror.

Chapter 7: Refraction: Bending Light and Bending Lives

1. Vera Nazarian, *The Perpetual Calendar of Inspiration* (Los Angeles: Norilana/Spirit, 2010).

2. Wikipedians, *Color,* https://books.google.com/books?id=UNUpe WbWVaYC&q=translucent+transparent+transmitted#v=snippet&q= ii&f=false.

3. Joni Eareckson Tada, "Why Do God's Children Suffer?" *Answers in Genesis,* May 27, 2009, https://answersingenesis.org/who-is-god /god-is-good/why-do-gods-children-suffer/.

4. Thomas Watson, *A Body of Divinity,* Kindle ed. (New York: Scriptura, 2015).

Chapter 8: Why Is the Sky Blue?

1. E. James Davis and Gustav Schweiger, *The Airborne Microparticle* (Berlin: Springer-Verlag, 2002), 5.

2. W. F. Adeney, "Sin Revealed by God," Bible Hub, http://biblehub .com/sermons/auth/adeney/sin_revealed_by_god.htm.

3. Dallas Willard, *The Spirit of the Disciplines: Understanding How God Changes Lives* (San Francisco: HarperOne, 1988), 230, emphasis added.

Chapter 9: Burn Bright

1. "Burn Bright" by Bernie Herms, Stephanie Rachel Lewis, David E. Moffitt, and Natalie Diane Grant, released October 15, 2015, on *Hurricane,* Universal Music Publishing Group.

2. C. H. Spurgeon, "Light. Fire. Faith. Life. Love," in *An All-Round Ministry: Addresses to Ministers and Students,* www.spurgeon.org /misc/aarm06.htm.

3. Spurgeon, "Light. Fire. Faith. Life. Love."

4. "M. William's Christian Testimony," TruthSaves.org, http://truthsaves .org/christian-testimony/m-williams-christian-testimony/. Reprinted with permission.

Chapter 10: LASER-Focused for the Lord

1. "Turning Up the Heat: Latest Evolution of Lockheed Martin Laser Weapon System Stops Truck in Field Test," Lockheed Martin, March 3, 2015, www.lockheedmartin.com/us/news/press-releases/2015 /march/ssc-space-athena-laser.html.

Chapter 11: We Must Have Oil for Our Lamps

1. D. A. Carson, "Matthew," in *The Expositor's Bible Commentary*, rev. ed., vol. 9, eds. Tremper Longman III and David E. Garland (Grand Rapids, MI: Zondervan, 2010), 552.

Chapter 12: Shining Brightly in a World of Brilliance

1. Park Benjamin, *The Age of Electricity, from Amber-Soul to Telephone* (London: Forgotten Books, 2013), 2–3. Original work published 1889. www.forgottenbooks.com/readbook_text/The _Age_of_Electricity_from_Amber-Soul_to_Telephone_10000 42611/13.

2. Jane Brox, *Brilliant: The Evolution of Artificial Light* (New York: Houghton Mifflin, 2010), 1–2.

3. Gaston Bachelard, *The Psychoanalysis of Fire* (Boston: Beacon Press, 1968), 55.

4. Brox, *Brilliant*, 295.

5. Brox, *Brilliant*, 296.

6. "Quick Facts About Global Christianity," Ockenga Institute, www .gordonconwell.edu/ockenga/research/Quick-Facts-about-Global -Christianity.cfm.

7. Ravi Zacharias, *Why Jesus? Rediscovering His Truth in an Age of Mass Marketed Spirituality*, Kindle ed. (Nashville: FaithWords, 2012), lc 68–70.

8. "Don't Blend In, Stand Out," Joyce Meyer Ministries, www.joyce meyer.org/articles/ea.aspx?article=dont_blend_in_stand_out.

9. Abby Stocker, "The Craziest Statistic You'll Read About North American Missions," *Christianity Today,* August 19, 2013, www.christianitytoday.com/ct/2013/august-web-only/non-christians-who-dont-know-christians.html.

10. Ray C. Stedman, "God at Work," RayStedman.org, 1963, www.raystedman.org/new-testament/philippians/god-at-work.

Chapter 13: No Lucky Stars, Just God's Heavenly Bodies

1. "Lucky Star," by Madonna, released July 27, 1983, on *Madonna,* Sire Records.

2. Ben Jonson, *Every Man Out of His Humour,* act 1, scene 3, opening line.

3. William Shakespeare, *All's Well That Ends Well,* act 1, scene 3.

4. William Shakespeare, *Hamlet,* act 5, scene 2.

5. Francis A. Schaeffer, *Francis A. Schaeffer Trilogy: The Three Essential Books in One Volume* (Wheaton, IL: Crossway, 1990), 266.

6. A. W. Tozer, *The Pursuit of God* (Seattle: CreateSpace, 2013), 7.

Chapter 15: No Half-Life

1. Ernest Rutherford, Uncyclopedia, http://uncyclopedia.wikia.com/wiki/Ernest_Rutherford.

2. Paul Vitello, "Taking a Break from the Lord's Work," *The New York Times,* August 1, 2010, www.nytimes.com/2010/08/02/nyregion/02burnout.html?_r=0.

3. "Pastor Burnout Statistics," PastorBurnout.com, www.pastorburnout.com/pastor-burnout-statistics.html.

4. Barna Group, "2015 State of Atheism in America," *Articles in Faith and Christianity,* March 24, 2015, https://www.barna.org/barna-update/culture/713-2015-state-of-atheism-in-america.

5. Dr. Kara E. Powell and Dr. Chap Clark, *Sticky Faith: Everyday Ideas to Build Lasting Faith in Your Kids* (Grand Rapids, MI: Zondervan, 2011), 15.

6. Pew Research Center, "Global Christianity: A Report on the Size and Distribution of the World's Christian Population," December 19, 2011, www.pewforum.org/2011/12/19/global-christianity -exec/?beta=true&utm_expid=53098246-2.Lly4CFSVQG2l phsg-KopIg.

7. Don Joseph Goewey, "85 Percent of What We Worry About Never Happens," August 25, 2015, *The Huffington Post,* www .huffingtonpost.com/don-joseph-goewey-/85-of-what-we-worry -about_b_8028368.html.

Chapter 16: The Inefficiency of Incandescence

1. Ernest Freeberg, *The Age of Edison* (New York: Penguin, 2014), 2.

2. Jane Brox, *Brilliant: The Evolution of Artificial Light* (New York: Houghton Mifflin, 2010), 206.

3. Natural Resources Defense Council, "NRDC Light Bulb Guide Updated in Time for Sunday's Start of 'Lighting Season,'" October 30, 2013, www.nrdc.org/media/2013/131030.asp.

4. "Honor Edison; One Minute Dark Tonight," *Chicago Tribune,* October 21, 1931, http://archives.chicagotribune.com/1931/10 /21/page/1/article/honor-edison-one-minute-dark-tonight.

Chapter 17: "Light Bringers" for a New Generation

1. Vincent Pieribone and David F. Gruber, *Aglow in the Dark* (Cambridge, MA: Harvard University Press, 2005), 24.

2. "Bioluminescence," Smithsonian, Ocean Portal: Find Your Blue, http://ocean.si.edu/bioluminescence.

3. Gary Lane, "From Darkness to Light: A Chilean Miner's Story," *CBN News,* October 30, 2010, www.cbn.com/cbnnews/world /2010/october/from-darkness-to-light-a-miners-story/?mobile= false.

4. Lane, "From Darkness to Light."

Chapter 18: The Lightning Flash

1. Ferris Jabr, "The Body Electric," *Outside,* September 22, 2014, www.outsideonline.com/1925996/body-electric.
2. William Shakespeare, *Macbeth,* act 1, scene 1.
3. Jabr, "The Body Electric."
4. Jabr, "The Body Electric."
5. Elisabeth Kwak-Hefferan, "After Shock," *5280,* January 2013.

Chapter 19: Celestial Light

1. Emanuel Swedenborg, *Arcana Coelestia,* ed. Rev. John Faulkner Potts (The American Swedenborg Printing & Publishing Society, 1920), 2:546.
2. William Wordsworth, "Ode: Intimations of Immortality from Recollections of Early Childhood," www.poetryfoundation.org /poem/174805?.
3. Louis Ginzberg, *The Legends of the Jews,* vol. 1 in *From the Creation to Jacob* (New York: Cosimo Classics, 2005), 37.
4. William Shakespeare, *King John,* ed. Dr. Barbara A. Mowat (New York: Washington Square, 2006), 119, act 3, scene 4, line 160.
5. "Meteorite Legends," The Meteorite Market, www.meteoritemarket. com/legend.htm; the snippets on this site were sourced from John G. Burke, *Cosmic Debris: Meteorites in History* (Oakland: University of California Press, 1986), 222–23.
6. Walter A. Elwell, ed., s.v. "Light," by Michael J. Wilkins, *Evangelical Dictionary of Biblical Theology* (Grand Rapids, MI: Baker, 1996), www.biblestudytools.com/dictionaries/bakers-evangelical-dictionary /light.html.

Chapter 20: The Brightest Magnetic Objects

1. C. H. Spurgeon, "The Marvelous Magnet," *Christian Classics Ethereal Library,* www.ccel.org/ccel/spurgeon/sermons29.xx.html.

2. Kerri Lenartowick, "Pope Francis: What Attracts Our Hearts 'Like a Magnet,'" Catholic News Agency, Aug. 11, 2013, www.catholic newsagency.com/news/pope-francis-what-attracts-our-hearts-like -a-magnet/.

3. Michael Faraday, *Experimental Researches in Electricity,* vol. 3 (New York: Taylor and Francis, 1846), 1–2.

4. Darren Walter, *The People-Magnet Church: Attracting Your Community to Christ* (Joplin, MO: College Press Publishing, 2001), 118.

Chapter 23: Earthquake Light

1. Friedemann Freund, quoted in Brian Clark Howard, "Bizarre Earthquake Lights Finally Explained," *National Geographic,* January 7, 2014, http://news.nationalgeographic.com/news/2014/01/140106 -earthquake-lights-earthquake-prediction-geology-science/.

Chapter 30: To Be Light and Shine Forever

1. Facts in this list are from "Wonders of Antiquity," Sacred-Texts.com, www.sacred-texts.com/eso/sta/sta14.htm.

2. "Livermore, California's Centennial Light," www.centennialbulb.org/.